DANGEROUS DAUGHTERS

Book by Nick Stimson

Music and lyrics by
Annemarie

‖SAMUEL FRENCH‖

samuelfrench.co.uk

For Amateur Production Enquiries

United Kingdom and World
excluding North America
plays@samuelfrench.co.uk
020 7255 4302/01

Each title is subject to availability from Samuel French,
depending upon country of performance.

THINKING ABOUT PERFORMING A SHOW?

There are thousands of plays and musicals available to perform from Samuel French right now, and applying for a licence is easier and more affordable than you might think

---

From classic plays to brand new musicals, from monologues to epic dramas, there are shows for everyone.

Plays and musicals are protected by copyright law so if you want to perform them, the first thing you'll need is a licence. This simple process helps support the playwright by ensuring they get paid for their work, and means that you'll have the documents you need to stage the show in public.

Not all our shows are available to perform all the time, so it's important to check and apply for a licence before you start rehearsals or commit to doing the show.

LEARN MORE & FIND THOUSANDS OF SHOWS

Browse our full range of plays and musicals and find out more about how to license a show
www.samuelfrench.co.uk/perform

Talk to the friendly experts in our Licensing team for advice on choosing a show, and help with licensing
plays@samuelfrench.co.uk   020 7387 9373

Acting Editions

BORN TO PERFORM

Playscripts designed from the ground up to work the way you do in rehearsal, performance and study

---

Larger, clearer text for easier reading

Wider margins for notes

Performance features such as character and props lists, sound and lighting cues, and more

---

+ CHOOSE A SIZE AND STYLE TO SUIT YOU

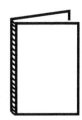

STANDARD EDITION

Our regular paperback book at our regular size

SPIRAL-BOUND EDITION

The same size as the Standard Edition, but with a sturdy, easy-to-fold, easy-to-hold spiral-bound spine

LARGE EDITION

A4 size and spiral bound, with larger text and a blank page for notes opposite every page of text. Perfect for technical and directing use

LEARN MORE | **samuelfrench.co.uk/actingeditions**

**Other plays with music by ANNEMARIE LEWIS THOMAS
published and licensed by Samuel French**

Around the World in Eighty Days with book and lyrics by
Phil Willmott

**FIND PERFECT PLAYS TO PERFORM AT
www.samuelfrench.co.uk/perform**

ABOUT THE COMPOSER AND LYRICIST

ANNEMARIE LEWIS THOMAS

Annemarie Lewis Thomas is a composer, lyricist and an accomplished musical director and arranger.

Full-length musicals include: in collaboration with Phil Willmott, Annemarie wrote the music to *Around the World in 80 Days, Uncle Ebenezer* and *The Wolf Boys*. In collaboration with Gerry Flanagan, Annemarie wrote the music and lyrics to *Great Expectations* and *Fool's Gold*. Other shows with Nick Stimson include *The Sunshine Gang, The Ballad of Kitty Jay, Just the Ticket, Celebs Anon* and *The Venus Factor*.

In collaboration with Daniel O'Brien she has written the original songs for seven pantomimes, three of which were commissioned for the Theatre Royal, Bury St Edmunds.

As the MD for the award-winning Steam Industry, Annemarie worked on all of the critically acclaimed BAC Christmas musicals. Other credits include: *Rent* (Olympia Theatre, Dublin), *Annie* (UK No 1 Tour), UK premieres *Victor/Victoria, Reefer Madness* (Bridewell), *Naked Boys Singing* (Madam JoJos), *Martin Charnin's 9 and a Half Quid Revue 9* (The King's Head).

In 2009 Annemarie opened The MTA (The Musical Theatre Academy) running the UK's first accelerated learning programme for performers. It was named as the School of the Year in The Stage 100 Awards in 2012 and 2017.

ABOUT THE AUTHOR

NICK STIMSON

Nick Stimson is a freelance playwright, theatre director and poet. He is also Associate Director of The Theatre Royal, Plymouth. Productions include: writer and director of *A Winter's Tale* (with the composer Howard Goodall) at The Sage, Gateshead and The Yvonne Arnaud Theatre, Guildford and Landor Theatre, London, (winner of Best Off West musical at the Offies 2014); *Sailors and Sweethearts*, a play about the artist Beryl Cook, at the Drum Theatre, Plymouth; writer and director of *NHS The Musical* (with music by Jimmy Jewell) at the Drum Theatre, Plymouth and the The Venue, Leicester Square, London; writer of *Hello Mister Capello* for the Palace Theatre, Watford; co-writer of *Promised Land* (written with Anthony Clavane) for Red Ladder Theatre, The Carriage Works, Leeds; writer of *Who Ate All The Pies?* (with music by Jimmy Jewell) at the Tristan Bates Theatre, London; writer of *The Venus Factor* and *The Sunshine Gang* (with music and lyrics by Annemarie Lewis Thomas) for the MTA at the Bridewell Theatre, London; writer and director of *Korczak* (with music by Chris Williams) at Theatre Royal, Plymouth, YMTUK at The Rose Theatre, London and Bialystok Opera Poland (international tour); writer and director of *The Day We Played Brazil* (with music by Chris Williams) for the Northcott Theatre, Exeter; writer of *Inventing Utopia*, a play about Dorothy and Leonard Elmhirst, for production at Dartington; co-writer (with Anthony Clavane) of *Leeds Lads* for Red Ladder Theatre at the Carriage Works, Leeds.

AUTHOR'S NOTE

Dangerous Daughters is the story of the radical suffragette movement, whose figurehead was Emmeline Pankhurst, told through the lives and actions of the three remarkable Pankhurst daughters: Christabel, Sylvia and Adela. It is a unique, extraordinary, passionate and in the end tragic tale; an important story that demanded to be told.

Behind the public facade, the Pankhursts were a family divided, a family at war. Christabel, the oldest of the three daughters, dedicated her life to the cause and let nothing, not even the pursuit of love and happiness, stand in the way of women's emancipation. Sylvia was an artist and the lover of Keir Hardie, the leader of the fledging Labour Party. By the end of the First World War Sylvia was estranged from the suffragettes, her own mother and Christabel, and Adela, the youngest, had been banished by Christabel to Australia.

The musical tells the story of their lives, loves, triumphs and tragedies set against the great events of the time. The rise of the suffragettes, originally seen as nothing more than a minor inconvenience by the male establishment, was marked by increasing militancy, violence, imprisonment, forced feeding and the death of Emily Wilding Davison under the hooves on the King's horse at the 1913 Derby. During the First World War, some suffragettes handed out white feathers of cowardice to supposed 'shirkers' in order to win what they saw as the greater battle – the emancipation of women. The musical culminates with the victory of the suffragettes and the disintegration of the Pankhurst family.

Nick Stimson and Annemarie Lewis Thomas
January 2018

MUSIC USE NOTE

CHARACTERS

EMMELINE PANKHURST – forties/fifties. A woman who has discovered her potential later in life. Strong. Brave. Dedicated. At times ruthless. Widowed.

CHRISTABEL PANKHURST – twenties/thirties. Eldest daughter and Emmeline's favoured child. Appears to be a strong, born leader but hides a fragile and conflicted inner self.

SYLVIA PANKHURST – twenties/thirties. Second daughter. An artist. A compassionate socialist. Lover of a much older man. True to herself and her beliefs.

ADELA PANKHURST – twenties. Youngest daughter. A fragile idealist often overlooked by her mother and sisters.

PANSY TUKE – twenties/forties. Leading member of the WSPU whose health was broken by the struggle.

GRACE ROE – twenties/forties. Leading member of the WSPU. Daughter of a wealthy family.

EMILY WILDING-DAVIDSON – twenties/thirties. Radical and driven member of the WSPU who threw herself under the king's horse in the 1913 Derby.

ANNIE KENNEY – twenties/thirties. Working class ex-mill girl and early member of the WSPU. Mercurial, enchanting and at times cruel. In love with Christabel.

FLORA DRUMMOND – thirties/fifties. Leading member of the WSPU. Organiser and disciplinarian known as the 'General'.

HELEN CRAGGS – twenties/thirties. School teacher who joined the WSPU. Romantically involved with Harry Pankhurst. A woman of compassion.

PRINCESSE DE POLIGNAC – thirties/forties. American heiress. Rich, decadent and lover of Christabel.

HARRY PANKHURST – twenties. Emmeline's often forgotten only son lost in a house of powerful women. A romantic.

Other characters:

SUPERINDENDENT WATSON
INSPECTOR MATHER
SIR EDWARD GREY
CHAIRMAN
JUDGE
POLICEMAN

PRISON WARDER
PRISON DOCTOR
OTHER MEMBERS OF THE WSPU
MEN AND WOMEN

Nick and Annemarie would like to thank Racky Plews, and the students of The MTA who helped develop the show.

The original *Dangerous Daughters* company of 2010:
Stef Booth, Erica Birtles, David Moss, Sam Hallion, Lauren Austin, Lydia Clarkson, Kay Victoria Hindmarsh, Laura B Mortemore, Ziggie Sky Ward, Karina Toolan, Bethan Forsey, Samantha Hull and Sarah Kappeler.

The *Dangerous Daughters* company of 2017:
Aiden Doyle, Alex Mellors, Anna Acevedo, Daniella Boyd, Ella Shipley, Emily Lyons, Erica Posadas, Lydia Gardiner, Georgina Young, Katy Southgate, Robbie Noonan, Laura Kent, Paris Hoxton, Amelia Williams, Tilly Beck, Hannah Stokes, Eva Solange Bortalis, Taylah Schofield and Mikulas Urbanek.

ACT I

Scene One

MUSIC 1: OVERTURE/PROLOGUE/THREE SISTERS

1903. A street in Leeds. **EMMELINE PANKHURST** *is addressing a belligerent crowd.* **CHRISTABEL, SYLVIA, ADELA** *and* **HARRY** *stand behind her.*

EMMELINE For the sake of all British women... For the sake of my daughters... In the name of sanity and sense women demand the right to vote!

SOLO

WHO'S THE FOOL? NOT US MY DEAR
OUR PURPOSE HERE IS VERY CLEAR

SOLO

TAKE CARE OF HOME

SOLO

TO NURTURE ALL

ALL

LOOK POLITICS IS NOT OUR CALL

SOLO

OUR FAMILIES TAKE ALL OUR TIME

SOLO

WE PROCREATE WHILST IN OUR PRIME

SOLO

WE COOK

SOLO

WE CLEAN

SOLO

TAKE CARE OF ALL

ALL

YES POLITICS IS NOT OUR CALL

EMMELINE

YOU MAKE THE POINT I'M TRYING TO MAKE
YOU SEW, YOU CLEAN, YOU EVEN BAKE
YOUR DAUGHTERS ALL SHOULD HAVE A CHOICE
TO HAVE A SAY,
TO HAVE A VOICE

The crowd heckle.

THIS IS OUR COUNTRY,
IT'S OUR DAY
WE MAKE A CROSS, WE HAVE OUR SAY

SOLO

WE'RE BUSY HERE

SOLO

PLEASE MOVE ALONG

SOLO

WE'RE FAR TOO WEAK

SOLO

OUR MIND'S NOT STRONG

MEN

YOU SILLY GIRL, PIPE DOWN (HOW QUAINT)
IT'S NINETEEN THREE, SHOW SOME RESTRAINT

EMMELINE *(to her daughters)* You must be unafraid and fight this battle.

To the crowd.

MY DAUGHTERS HEAR WHAT'S SAID IN FEAR

To daughters.

WE NEED A STRATEGY THAT'S CLEAR

To the crowd.

THE BATTLE CRY IS IN THEIR NAME

To daughters.

WE'LL WORK TOGETHER VOTES TO...

CHRISTABEL
CHRISTABEL

SYLVIA
SYLVIA

ADELA
ADELA

ALL THREE
PANKHURST THROUGH AND THROUGH
THREE DAUGHTERS BORN TO GREATNESS – TO STAGE A
    SOCIAL COUP
OUR FIGHT WILL BE RECORDED FOR ALL THE WORLD TO SEE
HOW WE, "THE PANKHURST SISTERS" EARNED OUR PLACE IN
    HISTORY

YET LEADERS ARE CREATED BY EVENTS THAT JUST UNFOLD
ARE THE PEOPLE LOST WITHIN THAT WHEN THEIR STORY
    GETS RETOLD?

CHRISTABEL
AS OFTEN WITH THE FIRST BORN I WAS THE FAVOURED
    CHILD
I LIVED THE LIFE MY MOTHER YEARNED – TO ALL INTENTS
    BEGUILED
BUT LIVING AS THE 'FAVOURED' ONE ADDS PRESSURE TO
    EACH DAY
I FOUND SALVATION TWICE A WEEK IN CLASSES OF BALLET

ARABESQUES AND PIROUETTES TRANSPORT ME TO AN AGE
WHEN A YOUNG GIRL LIVED THE FANTASY OF A LIFE UPON
    THE STAGE

MY BODY WAS THE VESSEL AS MUSIC COURSED MY VEINS
OH TO BE TRANSPORTED BACK – AS A YOUNG GIRL
    ENTERTAINS.

SYLVIA

MY FATHER WAS MY HERO – A PROUD AND UPRIGHT MAN
I LOVED TO HEAR HIS STORIES AS HE HATCHED EACH
    MASTER PLAN
MY MOTHER HAD MY SISTER – AS CONFIDANT AND FRIEND
I FOUND WITHIN MY PAINTINGS, A NEW WORLD I COULD
    TRANSCEND

BY LIVING IN THE SHADOWS I ADMIRED ALL THE SHADES
THE COLOURS OF MY PALETTE, MY ESCAPE FROM THE
    CRUSADE
AS ART IS ALL SUBJECTIVE – NOTHING'S EVER BLACK OR
    WHITE
TO LIVE WITHIN MY SKETCHBOOK LETTING FANTASY TAKE
    FLIGHT

ADELA

YOU WOULD THINK THAT AS THE YOUNGEST I WOULD LIVE A
    LIFE OF CHARM
DOTING PARENTS FUSSING ROUND, SIBLINGS PROTECTING ME
    FROM HARM
YET EACH PARENT HAD A DAUGHTER WHO FULFILLED
    PARENTAL NEED
AND EACH SISTER HAD A TALENT AND DESIRE TO SUCCEED

NOT SEEN OR HEARD I SKULKED AROUND UNTIL THE PENNY
    DROPPED
EMPOWERING GENERATIONS MEANT INJUSTICE COULD BE
    STOPPED
SO I BECAME A TEACHER
EVERY CHILD WOULD HAVE THE CHOICE
EDUCATION IS A POWERFUL TOOL TO UNLOCK THE
    YOUNGEST VOICE

ADELA *teaching in a school.*

PUPIL

BUT MISS WHAT IS THE ANSWER?

ADELA

IT'S MY QUESTIONING YOU'LL LEARN

THE ANSWER LIES WITHIN YOURSELF – NOW LET THOSE
    BRAIN COGS TURN

PUPIL

MISS PANKHURST!

ADELA

ALWAYS NEEDED

ADULT VOICE SO CLEAR AND STRONG

IT'S ONLY IN THE CLASSROOM THAT I FEEL LIKE I BELONG

The **THREE SISTERS** *and* **EMMELINE** *come together, with
ensemble backing.*

CHRISTABEL, SYLVIA, ADELA *and* **EMMELINE**

JUST AN EVERYDAY DESCRIPTION OF A FAMILY AT WAR

WE NEVER COULD HAVE GUESSED JUST WHAT THE FUTURE
    HELD IN STORE

FAMILIAL SCRIPT IS WRITTEN BY THE CHOICES WE ALL MADE

BUT A CHAPTER WAS STILL HIDDEN – THE BEST PLANS CAN
    GET WAYLAID.

Music 1 out.

Scene Two

1903. The parlour of **EMMELINE PANKHURST**'s *middle class home in Leeds. The* **PANKHURSTS** *prepare for a meeting.*

ADELA I am so excited!

EMMELINE Contain your excitement a little longer Adela and make sure the teapot is properly warmed.

ADELA Yes, Mother.

>   **ADELA** *exits to warm the teapot.*

EMMELINE Sylvia dear, would you be so good as to bring in the milk jug?

HARRY I'll get it.

EMMELINE Thank you, Harry.

CHRISTABEL My piano teacher says that giving women the vote will lead to anarchy and chaos.

EMMELINE That is because he is a man. *(Suddenly remembers)* We've forgotten the rich teas.

ADELA *(entering)* Teapot's warming.

HARRY *(entering with milk jug)* Milk.

SYLVIA There's some garibaldis in the cupboard.

EMMELINE Thank goodness.

CHRISTABEL Do you really think it possible that one day women will get the vote?

EMMELINE It is up to us to persuade the nation.

SYLVIA Just us...the Pankhursts?

EMMELINE From small acorns, dear. Shall we make a start?

>   *They sit. There is no chair for* **HARRY**.

HARRY I'll get a chair.

EMMELINE No, Harry. This meeting is for women only.

HARRY No chaps allowed? That's a bit rum.

EMMELINE I'm sorry, dear.

ADELA Surely our Harry doesn't count as a chap.

EMMELINE Run along, dear.

HARRY Righty oh. Fella knows when he's not wanted. Toodle pip. Chin chin, what!

HARRY *exits.*

EMMELINE I call this meeting to order. Sylvia, would you please take the minutes?

SYLVIA Of course, Mother.

EMMELINE Present... Emmeline Pankhurst, Christabel Pankhurst, Sylvia Pankhurst and... Adela Pankhurst.

SYLVIA *(writing)* 10th October 1903.

EMMELINE Let the City of Leeds become the birthplace of the first truly independent women's movement.

ADELA The day women changed the world!

EMMELINE Hush Adela, let us not get ahead of ourselves.

ADELA Sorry, Mother.

EMMELINE Who will take the chair?

ADELA You, of course, Mother. Who else?

EMMELINE No. Christabel will chair this meeting. She is the eldest. Come Christabel...the head of the table.

CHRISTABEL I don't know how to chair a meeting.

EMMELINE A girl of your abilities will soon learn.

CHRISTABEL *and* **EMMELINE** *change places.* **CHRISTABEL** *sits in the chair at the head of the meeting.*

SYLVIA That's where Father always sat.

EMMELINE This is what your father would have wanted...his wife and daughters rallying to a cause.

CHRISTABEL I call the meeting to order.

EMMELINE We have but one aim...the emancipation of British women.

CHRISTABEL The right to vote.

ADELA Hear, hear!

EMMELINE To be treated as equals.

ADELA Hear, hear!

EMMELINE Women's suffrage.

The...

CHRISTABEL Thank you, Mother. I think we all understand.

EMMELINE Yes, of course.

SYLVIA The Labour Party shares our beliefs. We must work with them.

EMMELINE It is a party run by men.

SYLVIA Good men, like Kier Hardie.

ADELA Not all men are against us. Tommy from down the road listened very attentively to my ideas.

CHRISTABEL Another of your infatuations?

ADELA *giggles.*

EMMELINE If we are to become a proper organisation then we need a name...

ADELA The Union of Right-Minded Women...

SYLVIA The Confederation of Women for Political Change...

ADELA Free Female Spirits Unite...

CHRISTABEL The Women's Social and Political Union.

EMMELINE Perfect!

CHRISTABEL The WSPU. Women demand the right to equality.

ADELA The unbreakable bond of sisterhood. Mother will be the first ever woman prime minister! You will be home secretary, Sylvia!

CHRISTABEL The rights of women.

SYLVIA Political change.

ADELA A dream come true.

CHRISTABEL The WSPU.

EMMELINE All agreed say aye...

ALL AYE.

MUSIC 2: "THE WSPU"

The **PANKHURSTS** *walk out into the world.*

CHRISTABEL
A PLAN IS FORMED WE MOVE ALONG
GOT PUT IN CHARGE, I MUST STAY STRONG
ALTHOUGH I'M SCARED, I CAN'T BE WEAK
TO FIND MY VOICE AND THEN TO SPEAK

MY MOTHER'S PUT HER FAITH IN ME
EACH FIGHT BEGINS WITH INTEGRITY

PANKHURSTS
THE PANKHURSTS STAND TOGETHER
THE PANKHURSTS STANDING STRONG
WE CAN'T IGNORE OUR PURPOSE
FATHER'S GONE
OUR FIGHT GOES ON
INJUSTICE IS OUR ENEMY
EQUALITY'S THE AIM
AND WHEN WE CHANGE THE LAW THEY WILL CELEBRATE THE
    NAME

1ST MAN Get back where you belong!

2ND MAN In the bloody kitchen! *(Both men laugh)*

SYLVIA
> EQUALITY IS WORTH THE FIGHT
> STAND UP AND SHOUT FOR WHAT IS RIGHT
> KNOW THINGS CAN CHANGE AS LINES GET BLURRED
> WE START TODAY CAN'T BE DETERRED

Music 2 under.

1ST MAN What was that all about?

2ND MAN God knows!

Music 2 up.

ADELA
> I STAND BESIDE MY SISTERS SHOUT EQUALITY FOR ALL
> WHERE GENDER'S JUST A WORD
> NOT THE SWORD ON WHICH WE FALL
> UTOPIAN IS MY VISION – FIGHTING FOR A BETTER DAY
> A MOVEMENT'S JUST THE START
> BUT AT LEAST WE'RE ON OUR WAY

1ST MAN
> Perverse!

2ND MAN
> Unnatural!

Over the song if needs be.

PANKHURSTS
> THE PANKHURSTS STAND TOGETHER
> THE PANKHURSTS STANDING STRONG
> WE CAN'T IGNORE OUR PURPOSE
> FATHER'S GONE
> OUR FIGHT GOES ON

Music 2 under.

FLORA Flora Drummond. Who's in charge here?

EMMELINE A new recruit, Christabel.

CHRISTABEL *(welcoming* **FLORA***)* I am Christabel Pankhurst. Welcome, Flora.

Music 2 up.

ALL WOMEN

WHO PUT THE MEN IN CHARGE?
SOME MOTHER SHOULD HAVE PUT THEM RIGHT
REFERRED TO AS THE MASTER RACE – WELL NOW
IT'S TIME TO FIGHT
NO LONGER JUST ACCESSORIES TO HUMOUR AND TO WOO

IT'S TIME TO NAME THE BATTLE
YOU JUST TRY TO TAME THIS SHREW

Music under. **PANSY TUKE** *and* **GRACE ROE** *enter.*

PANSY Pansy Tuke.

GRACE Grace Roe.

EMMELINE You will be ridiculed and abused by men. Are you prepared?

BOTH *(in rhythm)* YES.

Music 2 up.

ALL WOMEN

THE BATTLE LINES ARE DRAWN OUT – LET A SISTERHOOD
    DECIDE
IT IS TIME FOR FEMALE VOICES TIME TO BRIDGE THE GREAT
    DIVIDE
SO WOMEN STAND TOGETHER LET OUR MEMBERSHIP NOW
    SWELL
WE'VE HAD ENOUGH OF LIVING IN THIS MASCULINE-LED
    HELL

Music under. **EMILY WILDING DAVISON** *enters.*

EMILY I am Emily Wilding Davison.

Music up.

ALL WOMEN
> THE RIGHTEOUS CAUSE CAN'T FAIL TO WIN – SO VICT'RY IS IN
> SIGHT
> OUR MENFOLK MUST NOW RUE THE DAY WE ALL CHOSE TO
> UNITE
> OUR STRENGTH LIES IN OUR NUMBERS
> OUR ONLY OPTION IS TO WIN
> I STAND AMONGST MY SISTERS EACH OF US A HEROINE

Music 2 continues under. **ANNIE KENNEY** *enters.*

CHRISTABEL Who are you?

ANNIE Annie Keeney. From Saddleworth. Used to be a mill girl.

FLORA How delightful! A proper working class girl.

SYLVIA You are very welcome Annie.

ANNIE *(to* **CHRISTABEL***)* Heard you address a meeting. You inspired me.

CHRISTABEL Thank you.

ANNIE *(still addressing* **CHRISTABEL***)* I'm afraid of no man and I want to change the world.

CHRISTABEL *(going to her)* And that, my dear Annie, is exactly what we are going to do. *(Beat)* Now to plan. *(Beat.)* London is where the world turns, not Leeds, or Manchester. London. *(beat)* Sylvia, you will go on ahead and set up the London Headquarters of the WSPU.

SYLVIA What about my course at the Royal College of Art?

EMMELINE Now is not the time for selfish ambition. A great duty calls.

SYLVIA You expect me to give up my painting?

ANNIE I've given up my home and family to be here. What's daubin' a bit of paint on some canvas matter?

SYLVIA It matters to me.

ADELA What shall I do?

EMMELINE *(ignoring* **ADELA**. *To* **SYLVIA***)* As soon as humanly possible, Christabel and I will join you and take control of the organisation.

ADELA What about me? Shall I go to London with Sylvia?

EMMELINE All in good time Adela.

ADELA I could write pamphlets.

CHRISTABEL You heard what Mother said.

More women join them.

Are we ready? Forward!

Music up.

ALL

SO WOMEN STAND TOGETHER
SIDE BY SIDE WE'LL STAY SO STRONG
IT'S TIME TO CHANGE THE SYSTEM – AND TO RIGHT THIS
    AWFUL WRONG
A SIMPLE CROSS OUR MISSION
WITH THE BALLOT BOX OUR GOAL
THE WSPU ARRIVES TO PLAY A VITAL ROLE

Music 2 out.

MUSIC 2A: "THE WSPU" – Playout.

Scene Three

Free Trade Hall, Manchester, 1904. One **PLAINCLOTHES POLICEMAN, SUPERINTENDENT WATSON,** *stand watching the crowd.*

CHAIRMAN *(to the audience)* Ladies and gentlemen...it is a great honour to introduce to you a leading light of the Liberal Party, Sir Edward Grey.

CHAIRMAN *applauds as* **SIR EDWARD GREY** *stands to address the meeting.*

SIR EDWARD GREY Thank you. *(Beat)* Gentlemen, when the Liberal Party wins the forthcoming election, as it most surely will given the abject failure of the present Unionist government... **(CHRISTABEL** *and* **ANNIE** *enter quietly and demurely)* You are most welcome, ladies. **(CHRISTABEL** *and* **ANNIE** *take their seats)* As I was saying...when the Liberal Party wins the election and Mr Asquith forms his government, we pledge to immediately undertake sweeping reforms that are long overdue.

ANNIE Will the next Liberal Government give women the vote?

Uproar.

CHAIRMAN Order! Order!

Uproar subsides.

SIR EDWARD GREY As I was saying...we will bring into law sweeping reforms...

CHRISTABEL When will women be given the vote?

MUSIC 3: CHANGE THE LAW

Music starts.

ANNIE Answer us!

CHRISTABEL When will women be given the vote?

Uproar.

CHAIRMAN   *(to the* **POLICEMAN***)* Remove these women immediately!

ANNIE
WHY ARE WE A THREAT TO YOU?
WHY NOT SUPPORT OUR CAUSE

CHRISTABEL
JUST ONE REQUEST WELL OVERDUE

BOTH
IT'S TIME TO CHANGE THE LAWS

ANNIE
HALF THE POPULATION HAS A VOICE AS YET UNHEARD

CHRISTABEL
THE SITUATION BLATANTLY IS WELL

BOTH
SOMEWHAT ABSURD
THE RIGHT TO VOTE

WATSON
NOW COME ON GIRLS JUST MOVE ALONG

BOTH
WHAT ARE YOU SO FRIGHTENED OF PLEASE TELL?

WATSON
THE FEMALE VOICE JUST ISN'T STRONG

CHRISTABEL
NAIVE AND FOOLISH

ANNIE
GO TO HELL

CHAIRMAN
IT'S POLITICS – BEYOND YOUR REACH
YOU'VE EXERCISED ENOUGH FREE SPEECH

CHRISTABEL

>YOU PATRONISING LITTLE MAN

EDWARD GREY

>JUST MOVE THEM OUT, ENFORCE A BAN

CHAIRMAN

>UNBALANCED! SEE! THE FEMALE MIND

BOTH WOMEN

>OO STICKS AND STONES, YOU'RE SO UNKIND

WATSON

>GO DARN A SOCK, GO BAKE A PIE – THERE'S LOTS THAT YOU
>COULD DO

ANNIE *(simultaneously)*

>WHAT ARE YOU SO SCARED ABOUT?
>THE ALPHA MALE REVEALS SELF DOUBT

CHAIRMAN

>BUT POLITICS NEEDS THINKING MEN, THAT'S RIGHT
>THAT'S MEN – NOT YOU

Music 3 under.

The **OFFICER** *seizes* **ANNIE**. *She struggles violently.*

WATSON That's enough...

ANNIE Take your filthy hands off me!

CHRISTABEL *(with authority)* Let her go! I said let her go!

The **POLICEMAN** *lets go of* **ANNIE**.

WATSON I am an officer of the law and you are inciting a riot.

ANNIE We're not inciting any bloody riot.

GREY If you leave quietly, no charges will be brought against
you. *(Beat)* Do you understand? *(No answer)* I said do you
understand?

CHRISTABEL *steps forward and in a deliberate and controlled manner spits in* WATSON's *face. She turns to the* CHAIRMAN *and spits in his face too. She then returns to* WATSON *and strikes him on the mouth.*

WATSON Filthy creature

CHAIRMAN Arrest them both! Take them away!

WATSON *begins to hustle* ANNIE *and* CHRISTABEL *out of the meeting.*

Music 3 up.

CHRISTABEL
THE LAW IS MADE BY MEN, FOR MEN, NO WOMAN HAS
   INFORMED IT

GREY
REMOVE THEM ELSE THEY'LL START AGAIN

BOTH WOMEN
SHUT US DOWN? CHANGE THE LAW

CHRISTABEL
LOCK US UP AND YOU WILL SEE MORE WOMEN
STANDING SIDE BY SIDE

ANNIE
YOU'VE KEPT US MUTE FOR FAR TOO LONG

BOTH
EQUAL RIGHTS IS JUSTIFIED

Music 3 out. The WSPU *exit.*

Scene Four

CHRISTABEL *and* ANNIE *in separate cells waiting to be called into court for their trial.*

CHRISTABEL *(calling out)* Annie? Annie, can you hear me?

ANNIE I'm here Christabel...just the other side of the wall. *(Beat)* What will happen to us?

CHRISTABEL I don't know. *(Short silence)* This place...it smells of misery and despair.

ANNIE Stinks more like...stinks of sweat and poverty. Could do with a good scrub down with carbolic. *(Silence, then* CHRISTABEL *begins to sob)* We'll come through, Christabel... together we'll come through.

CHRISTABEL I'm frightened, Annie.

ANNIE What's there to be frightened of? They're only a bunch of self-important men. We'll bloody show 'em.

CHRISTABEL Never thought I'd find myself in a police cell. *(Beat)* I'm cold.

ANNIE I'm here, Christabel. I won't ever desert you.

CHRISTABEL Are you disappointed in me, Annie? Did you think I was a modern day Boadicea...a Joan of Arc? Did you think I'd burn at the stake and show no fear?

ANNIE No one's without fear. If they are they're mad.

CHRISTABEL You see Annie, I've always known it would be me who Mother would choose. I was the anointed one. *(Beat)* My mother...my sisters...they all think I'm strong...think I'm one who can bear the burden for all women. *(Beat)* But it's like a suit of armour I put on. The me that's inside is only flesh and blood.

ANNIE *(reaching out to touch the cell wall)* I'm here, Christabel. Can you feel me reaching out to you? I'm here.

CHRISTABEL Why must I always be the strong one?

ANNIE I want to hold you.

CHRISTABEL Did God ordain that Christabel Harriette Pankhurst should be the martyr? *(Beat)* My mother thinks that God might be a woman, but I know he's a man.

ANNIE *(softly)* I love you, Christabel.

CHRISTABEL What did you say?

ANNIE Nothing. *(Beat)* I'm shaking.

CHRISTABEL It's the cold.

ANNIE Yes. Yes of course it is.

Music 4.

MUSIC 4: HOLD MY HAND

CHRISTABEL
MY STRENGTH IS AN ILLUSION,
SMOKE AND MIRRORS, A DISGUISE
DESIGNED TO CATCH THE ENEMY OFF GUARD
THE MOVEMENT'S GROWN SO QUICKLY AND THE WOMEN
    LOOK TO ME
I HAVE NO CHOICE BUT TO INHABIT THIS CHARADE

I NEED TO FIND AN INNER STRENGTH TO GUIDE ME
A CORE OF STEEL IS NEEDED AT THIS TIME
IT'S GOOD TO HAVE A FRIEND LIKE YOU BESIDE ME

ANNIE
WE'LL STAND TOGETHER GUILTY OF THE CRIME
HOLD MY HAND
FEEL MY HEART

THE CONSTANT BEAT MADE STRONGER IN YOUR PRESENCE
EACH BREATH I TAKE IS DEEPER COS YOU'RE NEAR
I'M SMITTEN BY YOUR CHARMS, I HAVE NO DEFENCE
UNTIL YOU FEEL THE SAME I'LL PERSEVERE

WHEN YOU NEED SUPPORT YOU'LL FIND ME RIGHT BESIDE
    YOU
WHEN YOU NEED A FRIEND MY DOOR IS OPEN WIDE

I LOVE YOU IN A WAY THAT IS UNSPOKEN
FOREVER IN MY HEART YOU WILL RESIDE
HOLD MY HAND

BOTH

HOLD MY HAND

Music 4 out.

Music 4a scene change.

Scene Five

The court room. The JUDGE *looks down on proceedings.* SUPERINTENDENT WATSON *is in the witness box.* CHRISTABEL *and* ANNIE *stand in the dock. The public gallery fills with* MEMBERS OF THE WSPU: EMMELINE, SYLVIA *and* ADELA *among them.* HARRY *stands apart from the women and watches.*

JUDGE *(appalled)* She did what?

WATSON Spat in my face, your honour.

JUDGE *(disbelieving)* Spat in your face?

WATSON Yes, your honour. Miss Pankhurst then spat in the face of the chairman your honour.

JUDGE I am at a loss for words.

WATSON Then she struck me, your honour. Struck me about the mouth. Whereupon I arrested the pair of them.

JUDGE *(to* CHRISTABEL*)* Do you deny these charges, Miss Pankhurst?

ANNIE It happened like he said.

JUDGE I wasn't addressing you. *(Beat)* Miss Pankhurst?

CHRISTABEL I do not deny it happened.

JUDGE Had you lost your reason?

CHRISTABEL I never lose my reason or my temper.

JUDGE Then how do you explain your behaviour?

CHRISTABEL My conduct was meant as a protest against the legal position of women today.

The WOMEN *in the public gallery clap and cheer.*

JUDGE Quiet! I will not have this courtroom turned into a political demonstration.

CHRISTABEL We cannot make any orderly protest because we have not the means whereby citizens may do such a thing. We have not a vote, and so long as we have not votes we must be disorderly.

JUDGE Spitting? Striking police officers? Is that the way to gain the public's sympathy?

CHRISTABEL There is no other way whereby we can put forward our claims to political justice. When we have that you will not see us at the police courts, but so long as we have not votes things like this will happen.

Intro to ***"THE FIGHT GOES ON"***.

JUDGE Are you making a threat?

CHRISTABEL I am stating our case.

Music 5.

MUSIC 5: THE FIGHT GOES ON

WOMEN
> CAN'T YOU SEE THEY HAD NO CHOICE
> WITHOUT A VOTE THEY HAVE NO VOICE
> SIT IN JUDGMENT THAT'S YOUR ROLE
> BUT EXECUTE SOME SELF CONTROL
> THEY DID NO WRONG JUST ASK TO VOTE
> THEY'RE ON A CHARGE BECAUSE THEY SPOKE
> WE JUST WANT DEMOCRACY
> TO LEAVE A LASTING LEGACY
> LET THEM GO

Music 5 under.

JUDGE One more outburst of this nature and I will clear the public gallery! *(Court quietens)* Miss Pankhurst, do you realise the consequences of your actions?

CHRISTABEL What will be, will be.

JUDGE Miss Kenney?

ANNIE All my life I've been bullied by men, abused by men, hurt by men. I'll not bow my head to men a day longer.

JUDGE Very well. I find you both guilty of assault and obstruction. Miss Pankhurst I sentence you to a fine of 10s and 6d or, if you would prefer, seven days in gaol. Miss Kenney, I sentence you to a fine of 5s or five days in gaol. *(Beat)* I suggest when you have paid your fines you forget this campaigning nonsense, find yourselves husbands and settle down to live respectable, law-abiding lives.

CHRISTABEL I refuse to pay any fine.

ANNIE And me!

EMMELINE We will pay the fines immediately, your honour!

CHRISTABEL No!

JUDGE You realise what will happen to you if you do not pay the fine? You will be incarcerated alongside common criminals.

CHRISTABEL Then incarcerate us!

EMMELINE Christabel...

CHRISTABEL Mother...if you dare to pay my fine for me I will never come home again.

ANNIE We don't give a tinker's cuss for you or your flamin' male justice!

Music 5 up.

WOMEN
PAY THE FINE, ADMIT THE CRIME?
THEY WOULD RATHER SERVE THE TIME
GET A HUSBAND, SETTLE DOWN?
IT'S IN YOUR IGNORANCE WE DROWN
IT'S JUST MARTYRS YOU CREATE
AS YOU SEND THEM TO THEIR FATE
NEW SUPPORTERS WILL BE FOUND
YOU CAN'T RUN US UNDERGROUND
LET THEM GO

Music 5 under.

JUDGE *(furious)* Clear this courtroom!

Courtroom clears. **CHRISTABEL** *and* **ANNIE** *are taken away. The* **WOMEN** *step forward. Music 5 up.*

CHRISTABEL

ANNIE ARE YOU THERE? CAN YOU HEAR ME?
WHAT I'D GIVE TO FEEL HER TOUCH ONCE MORE
IMPRISONED ON MY OWN MAKES ME WONDER
WHY WHEN IT'S JUST US TWO I FEEL MORE SURE
YET WHEN ALONE THE DOUBTS BEGIN TO FESTER
SHOULD I BE THE ONE TO LEAD THIS FIGHT?
I FEEL THAT I'M NOT THAT STRONG
I DON'T KNOW IF I CAN CARRY ON
YET WHEN ANNIE'S HERE I KNOW THINGS WILL TURN OUT
    RIGHT

(to **ANNIE***)*

ANNIE ARE YOU THERE? CAN YOU HEAR ME?

(to herself)

WHAT I'D GIVE TO FEEL HER TOUCH ONCE MORE
IMPRISONED ON MY OWN MAKES ME WONDER
WHY WHEN IT'S JUST US TWO I FEEL MORE SURE
YET WHEN ALONE THE DOUBTS BEGIN TO FESTER

EMMELINE *(simultaneously)*

WHAT A PRICE TO PAY?
TO HAVE A SAY
SHE MADE HER CHOICE BUT STILL I WORRY
SHOULD WE HAVE FOUGHT A DIFFERENT WAY?

SYLVIA

CHRISTABEL YOU HAD A CHOICE
SAT IN JAIL YOU HAVE NO VOICE

ADELA

IF THIS IS VICTORY WHAT'S THE COST?
EACH PASSING DAY I FEEL MORE LOST

ANNIE

SAT ALONE YOUR MIND BEGINS TO WANDER
THINKING OF A PAST BOTH OLD AND NEW
SENSES REAWAKENING WITH EACH MEMORY
AND EVERY SENSE JUST LEADS ME BACK TO YOU
DEAR CHRISTABEL STAY STRONG, IF YOU CAN HEAR ME
I'M RIGHT THERE BESIDE YOU IN YOUR HEART
ONE DAY THIS WILL ALL BE DONE
AND THIS BATTLE WILL BE WON
THEN A NEW LIFE TOGETHER YOU AND I CAN START

WSPU *(simultaneously)*

NO GOING BACK
NO RETURN WE'RE ON THE ATTACK
THEY'VE RAISED THE STAKES, HOW HIGH WILL WE GO?

SYLVIA *(to* **WSPU***)*

YOU SAY HOW HIGH, BUT I SAY HOW LOW?

ADELA *(to* **EMMELINE***)*

MOTHER SEE I WANT TO FIGHT

EMMELINE *(to herself)*

WAS I WRONG, DID SHE CHOOSE RIGHT?

ADELA

YOUNGEST CHILD, UNSEEN, UNHEARD

ADELA/EMMELINE/SYLVIA

STILL WE CONTINUE UNDETERRED

WARDER Right then ladies...out you go.

WSPU

SO OUR HEROINES ARE FREE, THEY MADE THE SACRIFICE FOR
     ME
EVERY WOMAN NOW IN DEBT, ENSURE OUR CHILDREN DON'T
     FORGET
SO THE FIGHT GOES ON ANEW
NOW WE KNOW WHAT WE MUST DO
WE DEMAND DEMOCRACY
WE WANT A LASTING LEGACY

THE FIGHT GOES ON

Music 5 out.

Scene Six

London headquarters of the WSPU. SYLVIA *is writing a letter.* EMMELINE *enters holding a copy of the Daily Mail.*

EMMELINE The Daily Mail has coined a new name for us... 'dangerous and unstable suffragettes'.

SYLVIA Suffragettes? What sort of word is that?

EMMELINE 'suffragettes...' It says here...distinguishes us from 'the peaceful suffragists'. If they want to call us suffragettes then we will own that name and we will be proud of it. *(Beat)* I hope you're not writing to that man again.

SYLVIA If you mean Mr Keir Hardie...yes, I am.

EMMELINE I see.

SYLVIA Why do you dislike him so?

EMMELINE Liking has nothing to do with it. He is irrelevant.

SYLVIA Mother, he is the leader of the Labour Party. A national political force.

EMMELINE Come, come, Sylvia. Two members of parliament hardly qualifies as a national political force.

SYLVIA Ordinary working people support the Labour Party. One day they will form the government. *(*EMMELINE *laughs)* He is on our side.

EMMELINE He is a man.

SYLVIA You don't like him because he's working class...because he's rough around the edges. He intends to put a resolution before Parliament in support of women gaining the vote.

EMMELINE And the Liberals and Tories will laugh him out of Westminster. *(Beat)* Don't you understand...only women and women alone can win this struggle. *(Beat)* You are far too close to Mr Hardie. You appear to have forgotten he is a married man.

SYLVIA *(flaring)* How dare you insinuate...

ADELA *rushes in.*

ADELA Christabel's just arrived...says she's got a new plan.

EMMELINE Do calm down, Adela!

ADELA She's wearing this sash that...

SYLVIA Adela!

> **CHRISTABEL** *enters with a group of supporters including* **ANNIE, GRACE, PANSY, FLORA** *and* **EMILY. CHRISTABEL** *wears a sash of purple, white and green. Other sashes are distributed among the women.*

CHRISTABEL Purple for our dignity. White for our purity of purpose. Green for our everlasting hope. *(Beat)* Now, to business. Ladies, we have lobbied Members of Parliament and they have chosen not to heed us...we have attempted to speak with the Prime Minister but he slammed the door in our faces...we have marched, we have held mass meetings and we have been arrested and imprisoned for pleading our cause. The time has come for us to take direct action.

FLORA What's the plan, Christabel?

ANNIE Instruct us and we will follow you.

CHRISTABEL We will rush the Houses of Parliament.

SYLVIA Rush? What does that mean?

CHRISTABEL Exactly what it says. We will storm the Houses of Parliament and 10 Downing Street. All our strength... thousands of women driven by righteous anger...and we will force the Prime Minster to face us and give us the answer to our question...when will women be given the vote!

> *The* **WOMEN** *applaud.*

SYLVIA What has happened to you Christabel? What have you become?

MUSIC 6: THE DAILY FIGHT

CHRISTABEL We fight fire with fire.

SYLVIA The prisons will be overflowing with suffragettes.

CHRISTABEL They have left us no choice.

WOMEN
YOU THINK IF YOU IGNORE US WE'LL PACK UP AND GO AWAY?
WE HATE TO DISAPPOINT YOU BUT THIS CAUSE IS HERE TO
  STAY
NO MORE THE LITTLE WOMEN JUST CONTENT TO SIT AND
  WAIT
IT'S TIME FOR REVOLUTION
WHY NOT JUST NEGOTIATE?

CHRISTABEL To Downing St. Let's see what the Prime Minister
has to say to our faces when we beat down his door.

Music 6 under. The **WOMEN** *beat angrily on the door
of number 10 Downing Street.* **POLICEMEN** *intervene.*
FLORA DRUMMOND *bursts through the door but is ejected.*
WOMEN *shout and jeer at* **POLICE***. Music 6 up.*

WOMEN
YOU HAD YOUR CHANCE TO TALK THIS OUT YET STILL WE ARE
  IGNORED
WE'LL ESCALATE ACTIVITIES
YOUR TACTICS MEN ARE FLAWED!
OUR VOICE GROWS EVER LOUDER
DAY BY DAY IN STRENGTH WE GROW
UNITED BY A COMMON AIM WITH MEN THE ONLY FOE

Music 6 under. **ANNIE** *climbs up on a wall.* **POLICE** *try
to catch her. She dances away from them.*

ANNIE *(pointing at the* **POLICE***)* Look at 'em...frightened little
schoolboys...not seen a proper woman before... *(She hoists
up her skirts)* Want to look up me petticoats do you? Want
to gawp at me arse!

The **WOMEN** *laugh and cheer.*

FLORA Oh, you beautiful, irresistible blue-eyed beggar!

POLICE *pull* **ANNIE** *down from the wall. Music 6 up.*

WOMEN
WHAT'S THAT YOU'RE FEELING THREATENED?
HID BEHIND A WALL OF FEAR
COME OUT AND FIGHT YOUR CORNER IF YOUR VIEWS ARE
    THAT SINCERE
SMALL MEN IN NICE BIG OFFICES PROTECTED BY THEIR
    DESKS
COME OUT, DEBATE THE ISSUES, OR IS THAT JUST TOO
    GROTESQUE?

Music 6 under. **POLICE** *push the* **WOMEN** *back.* **FLORA**
DRUMMOND *picks up a stone and is about throw it at*
the window of 10 Downing Street.

SYLVIA Flora, there's no need for that!

CHRISTABEL *(picking up a stone)* There is every need!

SYLVIA Mother! Stop them!

EMMELINE *(picking up a stone)* We will make these men listen!

CHRISTABEL *hurls a stone at the window. The other*
women follow her example. **SYLVIA** *steps away from*
the others. **POLICE** *arrest the* **WOMEN** *who fiercely resist*
them. **POLICE** *throw them to the ground. Music 6 up.*

WOMEN
ARE YOU RUNNING OUT OF OPTIONS FOR THE TAMING OF
    THE SHREW?
DID YOU THINK WE'D JUST SURRENDER? ALCOTT'S WOMEN
    THROUGH AND THROUGH?
YOU ONCE TRIED TO HUSH OUR VOICES – NOW YOU BEAT OUR
    FLESH AS WELL
CAN'T YOU SEE THIS MAKES US STRONGER
HEAR THE EVER GROWING SWELL

Music 6 under. The WOMEN *are arrested and thrown into separate cells.* ADELA *enters.*

ADELA *(to a* POLICEMAN*)* I've come to hear Mr Churchill and Mr Lloyd George speak.

POLICEMAN You're not one of those fire-breathing suffragettes, are you, love?

ADELA *(smiling)* Do I look like one of those fearful creatures?

POLICEMAN All right, in you go.

The POLICEMEN *gallantly escorts* ADELA *to a chair.* ADELA *sits down and thanks him. She raises her hand.*

ADELA *(politely)* Mr Churchill... Mr Lloyd George...could you kindly inform the meeting exactly when your government plans to pass a law... *(stands, voice growing louder)* ...that will give the women of Britain the right to vote? *(The* POLICE *grab* ADELA*, arrest her, and throw her into a cell)* Mother... Christabel...look, I am one of you now... *(Beat)* Christabel? Did you hear me? I will suffer beside you.

CHRISTABEL You are a Pankhurst, are you not?

WARDER What is wrong with you women? A cross on a slip of paper? Is it really worth all of this?

ALL Yes.

Music 6 up.

WOMEN
JUSTICE IS SEDUCTIVE KEEPS US STRONG WHEN TIMES ARE
    LOW
WITH VICTORY IN SIGHT THE TIME IS CLOSE TO OVERTHROW
EACH MIRROR TELLS A STORY OF THE SUFFRAGE DAILY FIGHT
WE'RE IN THIS FOR THE LONG HAUL
DON'T REFUSE TO SEE OUR MIGHT!

ADELA *is thrown into a cell. Spotlights comes up all the* WOMEN *in their cells. A* WARDER *enters* EMMELINE's *cell.*

MUSIC 6: THE FIGHT GOES ON – Instrumental

SUFFRAGETTES
> THE FIGHT GOES ON
> THE FIGHT GOES ON
> THE FIGHT GOES ON

Music 6 out. Lights out on all the **SUFFRAGETTES.**

Scene Seven

A Manchester street, 1906.

Sound effects: sound of a **SUFFRAGETTE** *demonstration in the distance. Raised voices, distant shouts and cries.*

HARRY PANKHURST *enters. He chalks suffragette slogans on a pavement.*

Sound effects: **POLICE** *whistle blows offstage.*

HELEN CRAGGS *runs in. She is being pursued. She doesn't see* **HARRY** *and collides with him.*

HARRY Awfully sorry, old thing...you hurt?

HELEN No... I'm perfectly all right... I'm sorry... I didn't...

HARRY *and* **HELEN** ...see you.

They both laugh nervously. Short silence.

HELEN They're searching the streets... I must go...

HELEN *starts to go.*

HARRY You saw the suffragette demonstration?

HELEN I was in it. Policemen on horseback charged us. I saw women being trampled by the horses. It was horrible.

HARRY Not all us chaps behave like that, you know.

HELEN I know. *(Beat)* Please excuse me.

HELEN *starts to leave then sees the slogan* **HARRY** *has chalked on the pavement.*

Votes for Women. *(Beat)* Did you write that?

HARRY Yes.

HELEN Why?

HARRY Lots of men support the cause. Famous men too. George Bernard Shaw... HG Wells... Keir Hardie... *(Beat)* ...and me.

HELEN And you.

HARRY And me.

They look at each other.

Sound effects: **POLICE** *whistle blows again. Closer.*

POLICEMAN *runs in.* **HELEN** *suddenly grabs* **HARRY** *and passionately kisses him.*

POLICEMAN Here...that's enough of that kind of carry on.

HELEN *(breaking away from* **HARRY***)* Sorry officer...my young man, you see, he's in the Royal Navy... His leave's just about over...might not see him again for years.

POLICEMAN *(to* **HARRY***)* You a sailor then?

HARRY HMS Dreadnought. *(Beat. Imitating the guns)* Bang! Bang!

POLICEMAN *(smiles)* Just make sure you young people behave yourselves. *(Sees the chalking on the pavement)* Votes for Women. They're everywhere those bloody suffragettes. *(Beat)* Pardon the language, ma'am.

HELEN You think women shouldn't be given the vote?

POLICEMAN Shouting, breaking things, assaulting police officers. Still, not my place to think.

HELEN Perhaps they had reason to demonstrate. Perhaps it's the only way to get their message heard.

POLICEMAN You one of them are you? You a suffragette?

HARRY No. 'Course not. She's been with me all time. *(To* **HELEN***)* Haven't you, my dear?

HELEN That's right. All the time.

POLICEMAN If you want my advice you'll get off the streets quick as you can and go home. *(Sound of shouting and screaming in distance)* Excuse me.

The POLICEMAN *rushes off. Alone again both* HARRY *and* HELEN *are embarrassed.*

HELEN What happened just then...

HARRY I understand. Desperate times...

HELEN ...call for desperate measures. *(Beat)* I'm a teacher, you see. If I get arrested I'll lose my job.

HARRY Golly.

HELEN My name is Helen Craggs.

HARRY Harry Pankhurst.

HELEN Pankhurst?

HARRY Yes.

HELEN What...as in the Pankhursts? Emmeline and Christabel and...

HARRY Yes...that's me.

HELEN Good God! *(Beat)* Sorry.

HARRY I'm the little brother.

HELEN *(shaking hands)* How do you do, Harry Pankhurst.

HARRY How do you do, Helen Craggs.

SYLVIA *enters.*

SLYVIA Ah, there you are, Harry...we all thought you'd got lost or been arrested. It's carnage. Come along...

SYLVIA *turns to go.*

HARRY Sylvia, this is Helen Craggs. *(Beat)* She saved me from the police...

HELEN It was your brother who saved me actually, Miss Pankhurst.

HARRY We saved each other.

SYLVIA Delighted to make your acquaintance, Helen.

HELEN And you... Miss Pankhurst. *(Beat)* I'd better make myself scarce... *(Beat)* Goodbye Harry.

HARRY Goodbye Helen. *(Beat)* Perhaps we'll run into each other again.

HELEN Perhaps.

MUSIC 7: ROMANTIC NOTIONS

HELEN *goes. Music 7 starts.*

SYLVIA She's very pretty is Helen?

HARRY Is she? Can't say I'd noticed.

*SYLVIA goes. Music 7. We see both **HELEN** and **HARRY** in their own worlds.*

WHAT JUST HAPPENED THEN?
MY HEART MISSED A BEAT
DID I HALLUCINATE A SCENE AND MY TRUE LOVE I MEET?
WELL A DREAM OR NOT, LET EMOTIONS STIR
AND CUPID'S ARROW HIT THE SPOT THE DAY I FIRST MET HER

ROMANTIC NOTIONS FOR THE FIRST TIME
A SENSE OF OVERWHELMING JOY
NEW FOUND FEELINGS UNEXPLORED
A MAN EMERGES FROM A BOY
LOVE AT FIRST SIGHT CAN REALLY HAPPEN
I'M A WITNESS TO THAT CLAIM
COS I KNEW SHE WAS THE ONE FOR ME
WHEN I HEARD HER FIRST SAY MY NAME

TODAY THE WORLD HAS HIDDEN MEANING
NOT POLITICAL BUT TRUE
A NEW PAGE, A DIFFERENT SCENE, RING IN THE CHANGES I'VE
    MET YOU
AND THIS IS PUBERTY IN ACTION
MATURING AT A FRANTIC RATE

AT THE RISK OF SOUNDING FOOLISH,
JUST ONE KISS HAS SEALED MY FATE
SHE'S THE ONE FOR ME
MY DESTINY

HELEN

WHAT JUST HAPPENED THEN?
MY HEART MISSED A BEAT
I'VE NO TIME FOR A RELATIONSHIP MY LIFE'S COMPLETE
STUPID, CRAZY THOUGHTS
RUNNING THROUGH MY MIND
I CAN'T SEEM TO STOP THESE FEELINGS SINCE OUR PATHS
    ENTWINED

ROMANTIC NOTIONS INCONVENIENT
SEE THE TIMING ISN'T RIGHT
I'M A TEACHER OUT OF TRAINING
WHO HAS PLEDGED TO JOIN THE FIGHT
LOVE AT FIRST SIGHT IS AN ILLUSION
AND THESE FEELINGS SOON WILL PASS
I'LL JUST CARRY ON REGARDLESS, SURE THESE FEELINGS
    CANNOT LAST

BOTH

TODAY THE WORLD HAS HIDDEN MEANING
NOT POLITICAL BUT TRUE
A NEW PAGE, A DIFFERENT SCENE, RING IN THE CHANGES I'VE
    MET YOU
AND NOW THE ANSWERS COME MUCH QUICKER
AS THE QUESTIONS SOUND MORE CLEAR
THERE'S A PURPOSE IN MY LIFE AS INSECURITIES DISAPPEAR
(S)HE'S THE ONE FOR ME
MY DESTINY

Music 7 out.

Sound effects: the sound of rioting as **SUFFRAGETTES**
clash with **POLICE. HELEN** *exits.* **HARRY** *exits.*

Scene Eight

CHRISTABEL, EMMELINE, SYLVIA, ADELA, HELEN, GRACE, FLORA, PANSY, EMILY WILDING DAVISON and other WOMEN OF THE WSPU. All the WOMEN wear their purple, green and white sashes. They are an army going into battle. Some carry sticks and clubs while others hold stones. HARRY watches. Music 8.

MUSIC 8: THE WSPU – REPRISE

WOMEN
> THE BATTLE LINES ARE DRAWN OUT
> LET A SISTERHOOD DECIDE
> IT IS TIME TO RAISE OUR VOICES
> TRY TO BRIDGE THE GREAT DIVIDE
> SO WOMEN STAND TOGETHER
> LET OUR MEMBERSHIP NOW SWELL
> WE'VE HAD ENOUGH OF LIVING IN THIS MASCULINE LED
> > HELL

Music 8 under.

CHRISTABEL *(addressing the* WOMEN*)* The men who rule this country are arrogant and blind to justice. *(Beat)* Ladies, today we will make so much noise and cause so much destruction that even the most obdurate male will be forced to take notice! Are you ready, ladies? Smash their damned windows! Break down their blasted doors! Make *(beat)* them *(beat)* listen!

The WOMEN *cheer.*

Music 8 up.

The WOMEN *surge forward breaking windows and causing damage to government buildings.*

Sound effects: sound of riot and breaking glass.

WOMEN
> SO WOMEN STAND TOGETHER
> SIDE BY SIDE WE'LL STAY SO STRONG
> IT'S TIME TO CHANGE THE SYSTEM – AND TO RIGHT
> THIS AWFUL WRONG

POLICE *start to drag away the shouting and protesting* **WOMEN** *and throw them into the cells.*

> A SIMPLE CROSS OUR MISSION
> WITH THE BALLOT BOX OUR GOAL
> THE WSPU ARRIVES TO PLAY A VITAL ROLE

Music 8 out.

Spotlights come up on **EMMELINE, CHRISTABEL, SYLVIA, ADELA, HELEN, FLORA, EMILY, GRACE, PANSY** *and* **ANNIE** *in their cells in Holloway prison. The* **WARDER** *enters holding a metal plate with food on it.*

WARDER You are directed to wear prison clothing.

ALL WOMEN We refuse.

WARDER You will obey the law of the land or you will suffer.

ALL WOMEN We refuse.

WARDER You are ordered to eat the food you are given.

ALL WOMEN We refuse.

WARDER You cannot refuse!

EMILY It is our lives and we if we choose to starve ourselves to death in the name of women's suffrage, then that is what we will do.

A **DOCTOR** *and the* **JUDGE** *enter.*

JUDGE What in the name of God is wrong with these women?

CHRISTABEL We demand to be treated as political prisoners.

JUDGE Riot and damage to public property are criminal offences.

WARDER They are refusing all food, your honour. If this carries on much longer one of them is going to die.

JUDGE Are they insane?

DOCTOR No. They're not insane. They know very well what they are doing. *(Beat)* They are making themselves into martyrs. Every great cause needs its martyrs.

JUDGE I'll not have their blood on my hands.

DOCTOR *(to the* **WOMEN**. *Reasonably, calmly)* I am a doctor. It is my vocation and my duty to save life. You must understand that in refusing food you are putting us all in an extremely difficult situation. We cannot simply stand by and watch you starve yourselves to death.

The **WARDER** *thrusts the plate of food at* **EMMELINE**.

WARDER Eat.

EMMELINE *turns her head away. Silence.*

DOCTOR Very well, you leave us no choice.

The **WARDER, JUDGE** *and* **DOCTOR** *exit.*

SYLVIA *(reading aloud a letter)* My dearest Sylvia

MUSIC 9: "BUT WHAT IS LOVE"

How I admire your strength and your dedication to the cause

Yet I would be lying if I did not also voice my concern

I implore you to stop this hunger fight

I don't believe that this approach is yours

As yet we have never been able to walk hand in hand, but the possibility of that occurrence is tantalising

I would like you to live long enough to make this simple fantasy, our new reality

Your concerned and earnest love

Keir

Light fades on **SYLVIA** *and comes up on* **HELEN.**

HELEN

LOVE AT FIRST SIGHT IS AN ILLUSION
I SAW A BOY BECOME A MAN
I NEED TO FIND A QUICK SOLUTION
I NEED TO STOP THIS... IF I CAN
A DIFFERENT DAY, ANOTHER LIFETIME
MAYBE OUR HAPPINESS WOULD LAST
BUT WITH THIS FIGHT I'VE UNDERTAKEN
YOU'RE JUST A MEMORY IN MY PAST

Light fades on **HELEN** *and lights come up on* **CHRISTABEL**
and **ANNIE** *in separate cells.*

ANNIE *and* **CHRISTABEL**

A SPECIAL BOND THAT'S NOW UNSPOKEN
AN OPPORTUNITY NOW MISSED
AND SO I FOCUS ON TOMORROW
ONCE MORE THE FERVENT PRAGMATIST

Lights fade on **CHRISTABEL** *and* **ANNIE** *and come up
on* **ADELA.** *Simultaneously the* **WARDER, DOCTOR** *and
the* **JUDGE** *and others enter the cells. They force rubber
tubes down the throats of the* **WOMEN** *in order to force
feed them. It is violent and grotesque. The* **WOMEN**
*try to pull the rubber tubes from their throats. They
gag. Scream. Vomit. The food is forced into them. The
exhausted* **WOMEN** *fall to their cells.*

ADELA

I FEEL A HUNGER LIKE NO OTHER
MY SOUL IS CRAVING SOMETHING MORE
I TRY AGAIN TO PLEASE MY MOTHER
IT'S FOR HER LOVE I DO IMPLORE

Lights up on **SYLVIA, HELEN, CHRISTABEL, ANNIE** *and*
ADELA.

THE PANKHURSTS *and* **HELEN**
>BUT WHAT IS LOVE?
>IT CAN'T SURVIVE
>YOU FEED YOUR SOUL... TO STAY ALIVE
>AN INNER PEACE
>SOME ARDENT PRAYERS
>MY HUNGER'S FOR – THE ONE WHO CARES

Music 9 out.

WARDER They are jaundiced...pulses racing...another week of this and one of them is sure to die...

DOCTOR They will have only themselves to blame.

JUDGE There must be no martyrs. *(Beat)* Release them.

WARDER *(not understanding)* Your...honour?

DOCTOR If you release them they will immediately reoffend, be rearrested, found guilty again and thrown back into prison. The process of starvation will start all over again.

JUDGE Exactly. Cat and mouse, doctor.

DOCTOR Cat and mouse?

JUDGE We must always be one step ahead of these women. We will not allow them to starve themselves to death and become martyrs for their cause. Cat and mouse. Arrest. Trial. Incarceration. Then release them before they can kill themselves. We can repeat the process again and again. In the end we will break them. *(Beat)* Attrition, doctor. Attrition.

MUSIC 10: "CONVICTION"

That is how this war will be won.

Lights up on all the exhausted and frightened **SUFFRAGETTES** *as they stumble out of prison into the daylight. They are weak and ill,* **EMMELINE** *can barely stand. People shout insults at them.*

MUSIC 10: CONVICTION

EMMELINE

> THROW YOUR SCORN IN OUR DIRECTION
> I MEAN WE'VE HEARD IT ALL BEFORE
> DID YOU WANT TO THROW A FINAL INSULT
> BEFORE YOU SHUT THAT PRISON DOOR
> PATHETIC SHEEP JUST UP AND FOLLOW
> BUT WE'RE ALL SHEPHERDS NOT THE FLOCK
> WE HOLD THE KEYS TO JUSTICE
> WHILE YOU JUST BOLT THE LOCK
>
> SO PUT US IN YOUR PRISONS
> CAN'T YOU SEE IT MAKES US STRONG
> FROM THE MOMENT THAT WE LEAVE OUR VOICES JOIN THE
>   EVER SWELLING THRONG
> WHAT PRICE THE COST OF JUSTICE, IF YOUR SOULS YOU'RE
>   SELLING SHORT?
> THIS WAS ALL A PART OF A MASTER PLAN
> SEE WE HAD OUR DAY IN COURT

SOLOS

> WE GOT TO PROVE THAT WE WERE WORTHY
> WHEN WE HEARD THE BATTLE CRY
> A WORTHY CAUSE INDEED, A CAUSE FOR WHICH
> WE'RE PREPARED TO DIE
> SEE IT'S WORTH THE AGGRAVATION
> THOSE PRISON WALLS CAUSED US NO THREAT

ALL

> WE'RE PROUD TO HOLD THE TITLE OF A CONVICTED
>   SUFFRAGETTE
> SO THROW US TO THE LIONS, JUST LIKE DANIEL WE HAVE
>   LEARNT
> IF YOU PLAY WITHIN THE FIRE YOU SURELY WILL GET BURNT
> WE DON'T STAND HERE ALL DEFEATED
> STARING AT THE PRISON WALL
> FOR WE KNOW A THOUSAND OTHER WOMEN WILL JUST HEAR
>   THE BATTLE CALL

DOCTOR, JUDGE *and* **WARDER** *(simultaneously)*
> YOU SPEAK OF JUSTICE BUT YOU'RE ALL LAW BREAKERS
> THE SYSTEM SQUASHES REBEL TROUBLE MAKERS
> YOUR HUSBANDS WAIT FOR YOU AT HOME
> THAT IS YOUR PLACE YOU'VE HAD YOUR FUN
> CAN YOU NOT SEE THIS FIGHT IS DONE?
> YOUR FUTILE MISSION CAN'T BE WON
>
> BUT NOW YOU'VE HAD YOUR DAY, IT'S TIME FOR YOU TO SAY
>   GOODBYE
> ALTHOUGH YOU'RE FUGITIVES, IN TIME WE WILL FORGIVE
>   THE CRIME
> BUT NO MORE SACRIFICE
> PLEASE TAKE THIS GOOD ADVICE
> THIS BATTLE THAT YOU STARTED CAN'T BE WON.

SUFFRAGETTES *(simultaneously)*
> THROW YOUR SCORN IN OUR DIRECTION
> I MEAN WE'VE HEARD IT ALL BEFORE
> BUT OUR BATTLE CRY GROWS EVER STRONGER
> EACH TIME YOU SHUT THAT PRISON DOOR
> YOU JUST SIMPLY MUTE THE VOICES
> YET THE MESSAGE STILL RESOUNDS
> FOR EVERY WOMAN JAILED HERE
> A REPLACEMENT COULD BE FOUND
>
> SO THROW AWAY THE KEYS, BUT THE ISSUE WILL REMAIN
> WE'RE FIGHTING FOR OUR FUTURE
> NOTHING TO LOSE, BUT ALL TO GAIN
> YOU TRY TO SHOUT US DOWN, AND MAKE US VICTIMS OF THE
>   LAW
> BUT WE'RE NO VICTIMS, SIMPLY MARTYRS IN THIS
>   ESCALATING WAR
> THE FIGHT GOES ON

Music 10 out. The **DOCTOR,** **WARDER** *and* **JUDGE** *and others exit. Only the* **WOMEN** *remain.* **EMMELINE** *collapses.* **SYLVIA** *and* **ADELA** *go to her aid.*

SYLVIA Mother will not survive another spell in prison.

CHRISTABEL They may hurt us, they may force their feeding tubes down our throats and into our stomachs, they may shout their man-made laws from the rooftops, but they will never break us.

SYLVIA Didn't you hear me, Christabel? Mother will die if she goes to prison again! Other women will die!

CHRISTABEL No price is too high.

All but SYLVIA *applaud.*

SYLVIA The Labour Party... Keir Hardie...many men with progressive ideas are on our side! Let them help us!

CHRISTABEL I will not have our great struggle reduced to the level of some petty political squabble.

SYLVIA How can you be so blind!

CHRISTABEL If you are so fond of Mr Hardie and his Labour Party then I suggest you leave the WSPU and go to them. I'm sure he will continue to welcome you with open arms.

SYLVIA My life is my own!

CHRISTABEL No, Sylvia, your life should be the cause. Everything else is irrelevant. All our lives now have but one purpose... the emancipation of women...that and nothing else!

ANNIE You heard Christabel...bugger off! *(Nods towards* ADELA*)* And take that one with you!

ADELA You common little guttersnipe!

SYLVIA Adela!

Tension. Anger. HARRY *enters. He is laughing.*

HELEN What is it, Harry? What's happened?

HARRY The Prime Minister... Mr Asquith himself...has just announced that the Liberal Government will be putting a Conciliation Bill before Parliament. It's going to be in the King's speech! *(Beat)* It's the first step. You're on the road to victory! It won't be long now before you will have won the right for women to vote!

A moment of stunned silence and then wild celebration. **CHRISTABEL** *and* **EMILY** *do not join in.* **SYLVIA** *remains with* **EMMELINE** *who is very weak.*

EMILY *(loudly, stopping the celebrations)* How do we know we can trust Asquith? Men have betrayed us before and they'll betray again!

ANNIE Christabel?

CHRISTABEL The struggle is not yet over, but the situation has changed. *(Beat)* We will hold the government to their word. If they break their promise and there is no Conciliation Bill put before Parliament then Asquith and all his ministers will live to regret it. *(Beat)* But for now we will declare a truce. All militant activities will cease at once.

EMILY I'm not prepared to stop the fight!

ANNIE If Christabel says there is to be a truce then there will be a truce! Any woman who doesn't stand beside Christabel is a traitor!

EMILY I'm no traitor!

EMMELINE *(faint. Still very ill)* Do what my daughter asks of you...

SYLVIA Mother, don't wear yourself out...

EMMELINE Let us remember the price that has been paid. *(Beat)* All those women whose lives have been broken simply for demanding their right to vote. Their right to be treated as the equals of men. *(She falters.* **SYLVIA** *and* **ADELA** *support her)* Let us remember all the pain and indignities we have suffered. The blind hatred that has been poured upon us. *(Beat)* Let us remember the long days of imprisonment, the forced feedings, the lives that have been forever shattered. *(Beat)* The WSPU will do as Christabel instructs and declare an immediate truce.

MUSIC 11: ACT ONE FINALE – A NEW DAWN

ALL

IS THIS THE DAY?
CAN WE TRUST THESE MEN TO LET US HAVE OUR SAY?
THERE'S A RAY OF HOPE IN SIGHT
SHOULD WE CELEBRATE TONIGHT, OR SHOULD WE WAIT?
DON'T PLAY WITH FATE

AN UNCERTAIN TIME
IMPRISONED IN ONESELF BEFITS THE CRIME
THOUGHTS SUSPENDED IN MID AIR
IT'S TOO SOON TO JUST NOT CARE ABOUT THE FIGHT
STILL NOTHING'S RIGHT

YET WE HOPE IN DISBELIEF
OPTIMISM, A RELIEF
A GLIMMER OF LIGHT
WE STILL MUST FIGHT

THE RIGHTEOUS CAUSE CAN'T FAIL TO WIN – SO VICT'RY'S
    STILL IN SIGHT
OUR MENFOLK MUST NOW RUE THE DAY WE ALL CHOSE TO
    UNITE
OUR STRENGTH LIES IN OUR NUMBERS
OUR ONLY OPTION IS TO WIN
I STAND AMONGST MY SISTERS EACH OF US A HEROINE

Music 11 out. Lights out on ACT I.

ACT II

Scene Nine

1908. The night before the opening of Parliament. A **WSPU** *celebration party in anticipation of the king's speech and the third reading of the Conciliation Bill.*

MUSIC 12: "THE CHAMPAGNE WALTZ".

Two couples are dancing, **CHRISTABEL** *with* **ANNIE** *and* **HELEN** *with* **HARRY**. **SYLVIA, ADELA** *and other* **MEMBERS OF THE WSPU** *stand watching and talking as they drink champagne.*

ANNIE *(as they dance)* I feel like Cinderella dancing at the ball. Do you like me crystal slippers?

CHRISTABEL Am I your fairy godmother then?

ANNIE No. You're my beautiful princess. *(Beat. Looks towards* **SYLVIA** *and* **ADELA***)* Look, there's the ugly sisters!

CHRISTABEL *and* **ANNIE** *laugh and then dance away.*

HELEN *(as they dance)* Seems like I'm living in a dream.

HARRY How's that?

HELEN Leaving school teaching. Working for the WSPU. Rubbing shoulders with the infamous Pankhursts.

HARRY Let's both of us live in the same dream.

HELEN Harry, you mustn't misunderstand...

HARRY *(gently hushing her)* Shhh...just dance with me...

HELEN *and* **HARRY** *dance away. The waltz comes to an end. Music 12 out. The dancers and others applaud.*

EMMELINE *enters carrying a copy of The Times.*

EMMELINE Here it is, ladies! Hot off the press. Tomorrow's Times. The King's Speech. It will announce the third reading of the Conciliation Bill.

Shouts and applause.

GRACE What does it say?

ANNIE Time for all that later...tonight's for dancing...another waltz...

CHRISTABEL No. Read it to us.

EMMELINE *opens the newspaper and scans through the King's speech.*

EMMELINE South Africa...foreign powers...Japanese government... Persia... India...trade... Old age pensions... Poor relief...sickness and invalidity insurance... *(Silence.* **EMMELINE** *looks up)* No mention of the third reading of the Conciliation Bill.

Silence.

EMILY The prime minister has reneged on his promise.

PANSY Taken us so far...made us believe he would support us... then dropped us.

FLORA We have been betrayed.

GRACE *(looking to* **CHRISTABEL***)* What are we to do?

CHRISTABEL *hesitates.*

FLORA Christabel?

EMILY Tell us, Christabel? Lead us.

Silence. **CHRISTABEL** *still hesitates.*

ANNIE *(desperately)* There's no need to stop the party. Let's enjoy ourselves tonight, eh? We can worry about the Conciliation Bill tomorrow. Tonight let's dance. Laugh. Drink. Live. Love. (**ANNIE** *fills a glass with champagne and drinks it down. She laughs*) Never had champagne before. It's wonderful. It really does tickle your nose. (**ANNIE** *goes to* **CHRISTABEL***) Strike up the band. Let's dance the night away!

CHRISTABEL *moves away from* **ANNIE**.

CHRISTABEL Asquith and his government have lied to us. All they wanted was to keep us quiet. *(Beat)* From now on the WSPU will be more militant, louder, more dangerous than we ever were before. The truce is over. (**SUFFRAGETTES**, *except for* **ANNIE** *and* **SYLVIA**, *cheer and applaud.*) The WSPU will press forward, ready to sacrifice ourselves even unto death if need be, in the cause of women's freedom!

EMILY Even unto death!

More applause and cheering.

ANNIE One more dance... Christabel...

CHRISTABEL No more dancing. *(Beat)* We will attack these lying politicians with every means at our disposal. With our fists, with sticks and stones, with whips and with fire. We will confront them in their homes and in their churches. We will attack them as they walk in the street. We will smash the windows of their offices, their gentlemen's clubs, their hotels and department stores. Let the men of Britain wake up to the sound of breaking glass! We will pour acid, ink and tar into their post boxes. We will dig up their precious golf courses. We will burn down their houses!

MUSIC 13: "VOTES FOR WOMEN". Music under. The **WOMEN** *march into action.* **SYLVIA** *and* **ADELA** *hesitate.* **HARRY** *tries to stop* **HELEN** *from leaving.*

HELEN I must go with them.

HARRY Let me come with you.

HELEN You know you can't.

HARRY Then for God's sake be careful.

HELEN kisses HARRY and then joins the WOMEN. The SUFFRAGETTES turn and look at SYLVIA and ADELA.

SYLVIA *(to ADELA)* There are other ways of changing the world.

ADELA I am a Pankhurst. My place is with them.

ADELA breaks away from SYLVIA and runs downstage to join the other WOMEN.

CHRISTABEL Sylvia?

Reluctantly SYLVIA joins the WOMEN.

EMMELINE Are we ready, ladies?

CHRISTABEL Go to it!

The SUFFRAGETTES proceed to smash windows and cause havoc. They strike POLICEMEN and are more violent than ever before.

Sound effects: breaking glass followed by rioting.

Music 13 up.

ALL
WE SAID THAT WE'D TAKE ACTION NOW THERE'S NOTHING
    LEFT TO CHOOSE
BEFORE YOU MAKE A JUDGEMENT WALK A MILE IN WOMEN'S
    SHOES
POLITICIANS MOVING GOALPOSTS NEVER CENTRE, LEFT OR
    RIGHT
NOW RHETORIC JUST BORES US SO WE SAY IT'S TIME TO
    FIGHT.

Music 13 under. SYLVIA walks away from CHRISTABEL and the others.

SYLVIA This has become wanton destruction without purpose! It must stop!

CHRISTABEL Now we know exactly where you stand.

SYLVIA What do you mean?

ANNIE You've never really been one of us. You're just a bloody socialist.

EMILY Prison...hunger strikes...they are not enough...we must sacrifice our lives for the cause!

FLORA Spoken like a true suffragette!

Other WOMEN *cheer.*

SYLVIA Go to the East End. There you'll find poor women crammed into slum dwellings...whole families...ten to a room...underfed...unemployed...children dying of diphtheria...

CHRISTABEL There can be no distractions from the cause. It is time you went, Sylvia.

SYLVIA *(turning to* ADELA*)* Adela...make up your own mind...

ADELA *wavers. She steps towards* SYLVIA.

FLORA Get back in line!

EMMELINE Remember who you are.

SYLVIA Adela...

ADELA *wavers.*

FLORA Back in line, I said...

ANNIE We don't need her... she hasn't got the heart for this.

ADELA *(flaring at* ANNIE*)* I'm not afraid of you!

ANNIE *laughs.* ADELA *joins the other* SUFFRAGETTES.

EMMELINE Enough! *(Beat)* We must stand strong. Ladies, are you prepared to take the consequences of your actions?

The **WOMEN** *cheer.* **ADELA** *is frightened.* **SYLVIA** *exits.*
HARRY *watches. Music 13 up.*

ALL

> BEAT US, STARVE US, KILL US, WHAT'S THE WORST THAT YOU
>   COULD DO?
> WE ACT WITH ALL GOOD CONSCIENCE – IS THAT THE SAME
>   FOR YOU?
> MORE WOMEN DAILY JOIN US – SEE OUR ARMY GROWS MORE
>   STRONG
> WE'RE FIGHTING POLITICIANS AND WE'RE RIGHTING ONE
>   GREAT WRONG

Music 13 under. **ADELA** *is frightened and sobbing.*

ANNIE Look at her. Mithering like a baby. She's not made of the same stuff as Christabel and Emmeline! She don't deserve to bear the Pankhurst name!

ADELA *(furious. Sobbing.)* How dare you! You upstart... you common little mill girl...you're nothing...you destroy everything I ever loved...

ANNIE Nobody respects her! Nobody wants her here!

> **ADELA** *attacks* **ANNIE.** *Others pull* **ADELA** *away.*

ANNIE She's unbalanced...she's crazy!

ADELA I'm a Pankhurst! I'll say and do as I think!

CHRISTABEL *(to* **ADELA***)* Adela, you must go.

ADELA Mother, no...don't let her...

CHRISTABEL You are no longer useful to the cause.

ADELA *(desperate)* Please... Mother...

CHRISTABEL You are a distraction, an embarrassment to the WSPU. *(Beat)* Go!

EMMELINE You heard what Christabel said.

ADELA But, Mother...

EMMELINE I will come to you later. *(Beat)* Go now, child.

ANNIE Go.

Distraught and sobbing **ADELA** *leaves the* **WOMEN**. *The* **POLICE** *enter.*

POLICEMAN In the King's name I order this assembly to disperse immediately.

The **WOMEN** *tie their hands together with ropes and chains until all are manacled and bound.*

EMILY *(shouts to the* **POLICE***)* Come on, then! Attack us, you brave men! Do your worst! We welcome death!

HELEN Deeds not words!

POLICE *wade into the chained and manacled* **WOMEN** *and beat them.* **HARRY** *rushes into the fray but is beaten back. Screams and angry shouting. The* **POLICE** *retreat leaving the* **WOMEN** *beaten and bleeding.*

POLICEMAN I arrest you for assault.

GRACE It is a woman's right to live as she wants to live...

POLICEMAN Riot.

ANNIE To love as she wants to love...

POLICEMAN Affray.

FLORA To be herself...

POLICEMAN Violent disorder.

EMILY To know herself...

POLICEMAN Criminal damage.

EMMELINE To walk in fear of no man.

POLICEMAN Grievous bodily harm.

CHRISTABEL To cast her vote.

Pause.

Music 13 up. The bloodied and battered **WOMEN** *sing. They remain dignified and proud.*

ALL

FIGHT FOR GENERATIONS – FOR A WORLD AS YET UNBORN
AND IN THEIR NAME WE'LL DIE – TO SEE A LIBERATED DAWN
EMERGING FROM THE DARKNESS – VICTORIOUS IN OUR
    FIGHT
WE STILL SAY VOTES FOR WOMEN – AND THE END IS IN OUR
    SIGHT

Music 13 out. The **SUFFRAGETTES** *exit.* **ADELA** *and* **HARRY** *exit.*

MUSIC 14: SCENE CHANGE.

Scene Ten

SYLVIA *in her attic studio in London. There is an easel and paints and a blank canvas.* SYLVIA *is tidying up. She looks happy and expectant. A knock at the door.* SYLVIA *quickly runs her fingers through her hair and straightens her dress. She opens the door. A poor and ragged East End woman stands there.* SYLVIA *is clearly disappointed.*

WOMAN You said to come round this morning. You said you wanted to paint me picture. You said you'd pay me a bob if I sat for you. *(Beat)* What's wrong, love? Look like you lost a quid and found a farthin'.

SYLVIA I'm sorry...do come in.

The WOMAN *enters and looks warily around the studio.*

WOMAN Expectin' someone else was you?

SYLVIA *(going to her easel and paints)* On that stool over there, please.

WOMAN *(going to the stool)* Not takin' me clothes off, not for you, not for no one.

SYLVIA No. Just as you are. *(Beat)* Please sit down. *(The* WOMAN *sits)* Now look at me. That's right. Head up a bit. Three quarters on...that's it. Perfect.

WOMAN A bob, you said.

SYLVIA Yes, a shilling. *(*SYLVIA *starts to sketch)* Please sit still.

SYLVIA *continues drawing.*

WOMAN You're that Sylvia Pankhurst woman, aren't ya?

SYLVIA Try not to fidget. Be as still as possible.

WOMAN All that votes for women m'larky. *(Beat)* What's getting the vote going to do for me, eh?

SYLVIA *(as she draws)* Don't you want a say in who governs you? Do you think it should be left to men and men alone to decide a woman's future?

WOMAN Listen love, my husband's a docker. Royal Albert. Took a tumble three months back and ain't worked since. That's why I'm sittin' here on me arse letting you do me picture. Got six kids. Think I've got the time on me hands to go out there demonstatin'? Think again, love.

SYLVIA Try to be still.

Music 15.

MUSIC 15: PORTRAIT OF SYLVIA

SEE EACH WOMAN'S STORY BY THE LINES ETCHED ON HER
    FACE
I TRY TO DRAW THE PORTRAIT AS HER HIST'RY I RETRACE
EACH HAS A DIFF'RENT LIGHTNESS AS THE SHADOWS START
    TO FALL
TRY TO CAPTURE EV'RY NUANCE WITH MY PALETTE I
    RECALL

DOES ART IMITATE LIFE?
BEHIND EACH PORTRAIT SITS A MOTHER, SISTER, WIFE
THE RESOLUTION IN HER EYES – TO SEE A SYSTEM
    MODERNISE
FIGHTING FOR A FUTURE YET TO BE

EVERY PORTRAIT IS A SNAPSHOT OF A SPECIAL TIME AND
    PLACE
WILL HISTORY EXULT THEM OR REVILE THEM AS
    DISGRACED?
EACH PICTURE TELLS THE STORY OF CONVICTIONS STRONG
    AND TRUE
SEE HOW STRENGTH LIES IN THE CONTRAST OF EACH
    COLOURS VIBRANT HUE

DOES LIFE IMITATE ART?
DOES THE WISDOM OF THEIR SOUL THIS LOOK IMPART?

> STEELY LOOK AND FATEFUL GLARE – SHOWS THE WORLD
>   HOW MUCH THEY CARED
> FIGHTING FOR A FUTURE YEARNED TO SEE
>
> NEXT I DRAW MY FACE, MY OWN PATH RETRACE
>   IMPERFECTIONS MAGNIFIED
> AS I FIGHT MY CONCENTRATION IT'S WITH SELF
>   DEPRECIATION MY REFLECTION'S PERSONIFIED

Music 15 out.

A knock at the door. **SYLVIA** *puts down her brush and hurriedly tidies herself up. She opens the door. Again her disappointment is obvious when she sees that it is* **CHRISTABEL. CHRISTABEL** *sweeps in.*

SYLVIA What do you want?

CHRISTABEL So this is your famous studio.

SYLVIA Why are you here?

CHRISTABEL Are you still consorting with that man?

SYLVIA If you mean Mr Hardie, then the answer is yes. *(Beat)* He's calling on me this morning. I thought it was him when you knocked.

CHRISTABEL Unsavoury gossip undermines the cause.

SYLVIA If that's what you came to tell me you can leave now.

CHRISTABEL I came to ask you whose side are you on, Sylvia?

SYLVIA The side of the poor and disenfranchised. The side you should be on.

CHRISTABEL If you cannot put the cause of women's suffrage before all else then I think it best for all concerned if you adopt a lower profile.

SYLVIA Are you expelling me from the WSPU?

CHRISTABEL It's all a question of how best to serve the cause.

SYLVIA Whose cause, Christabel? Womankind or yours?

CHRISTABEL Your views and behaviour can no longer be tolerated.

SYLVIA We are sisters.

CHRISTABEL I have many sisters now. *(She glances at the sketch)* It is a fair likeness. You have talent. *(Beat)* Good day.

CHRISTABEL *exits. Pause.*

WOMAN Can I move yet? Me bloody arse has gone numb.

SYLVIA Sorry. *(SYLVIA takes some change from her purse and gives it to the WOMAN)* Here. I won't be needing you anymore today.

WOMAN That's two bob.

SYLVIA Take it, please.

WOMAN You ain't got to ask twice, love. *(Laughing)* Votes for women!

The WOMAN *exits. Music 15 returns.*

MUSIC 15: PORTRAIT OF SYLVIA – continues

SYLVIA

FRAME THE PAST SUSPEND TIME
FORGET THE PERSON FOR NARRATION OF THEIR CRIME
EACH ONE A HERO OF HER DAY
TO CAST HER VOTE – JUST HAVE HER SAY
FIGHTING FOR A WORLD WE FELT SHOULD BE

THAT WOMAN'S ME.

Music 15 out. Lights fade on SYLVIA.

Scene Eleven

A small, plain room in a boarding house in Wemyss Bay, Scotland. ADELA *enters carrying her suitcase. She hesitates and then looks out of the window. She is unwell and on the verge of a major breakdown. Music 16.*

MUSIC 16: VOTE ADELA

ADELA

YOU WOULD THINK THAT AS THE YOUNGEST I WOULD LIVE A
    LIFE OF CHARM
DOTING PARENTS FUSSING ROUND – SIBLINGS PROTECTING
    ME FROM HARM
WHAT A JOKE!
SENT AWAY!
BUT I'M A PANKHURST TILL THE DAY I DIE
WHY NOT ME MOTHER? CAN'T YOU SEE MOTHER? NO
    REPRIEVE FOR THE YOUNGEST CHILD

WHERE DID TOMORROW GO?
ASPIRATIONS STOLE AWAY
THE PAST THAT BROUGHT ME HERE SEEMS TO THINK
THAT I'VE OUTSTAYED MY WELCOME
PATRONISED, THEN OSTRACISED,
IS THAT THE WAY TO TREAT YOUR OWN?
SURROUNDED BY THE MASSES – YET YOU LEAVE YOUR CHILD
    ALONE

IF FATHER WAS STILL HERE WOULD THINGS BE DIFFERENT?
WOULD HE LISTEN TO MY VOICE ABOVE THE THRONG?
WOULD HE OFFER AN OPINION ON THE PATH I CHOSE TO
    TAKE?
OR LIKE MOTHER WOULD HE THINK THAT I CHOSE WRONG?
    ALL WRONG

HUSH ADELA, NO ADELA
MAYBE SHE'S NOT WELL
A PROBLEM CHILD – TOO MEEK AND MILD
NOT A FIGHTER LIKE HER SISTER CHRISTABEL – OH POOR
    ADELA!

THIS IS ME.... JUST ME
JUST A BROKEN SOUL EXPOSED FOR ALL TO SEE

YOU WOULD THINK THAT AS THE YOUNGEST
YOU WOULD THINK THAT AS A PERSON
VOTES FOR WOMEN – VOTE ADELA
I AM ME!

Music 16 out. EMMELINE *enters.* ADELA *is surprised and overwhelmed.* EMMELINE *inspects the room.*

You came.

EMMELINE I said I would. *(Beat)* Simple but adequate.

ADELA It's damp. Mildew. Miles from anywhere.

EMMELINE Many a woman occupying a prison cell would gladly exchange with you. *(Silence)* You understand why you have been sent here, Adela? *(Beat)* Your attack on poor Annie was unwarranted.

ADELA I did not think so.

EMMELINE Your behaviour has become erratic and unpredictable. Everyone has been worried about you.

ADELA My nerves have been on edge. I'm feeling much better now.

EMMELINE The Scottish air is so bracing. It has restorative powers. *(Offering* ADELA *a package)* I've brought you some garibaldis. I know you like them.

ADELA I don't want garibaldis. I want to go back to London.

EMMELINE There are some charming walks around the bay. A few weeks in the countryside and you'll soon be your old self again.

ADELA Why have I been banished?

EMMELINE No need to be so dramatic, my dear child. You have not been banished. Christabel and I have your best interests at heart.

ADELA Then let me come back to London...let me come home
with you.

Silence.

EMMELINE Would you describe yourself as a socialist, like Sylvia?

ADELA I do not know.

EMMELINE *(impatiently)* Come, come child...everyone knows
what they are. Are you a socialist?

ADELA I am a suffragette...

EMMELINE Christabel and I feel it is time you found a purpose
in your life.

ADELA My work for the WSPU is my purpose.

EMMELINE Some sort of meaningful activity that best suits
your talents.

ADELA I don't understand?

EMMELINE Let me be plain. *(Beat)* What type of work would
you like to do?

ADELA Please, Mother...

EMMELINE What type of work?

Silence.

ADELA I do not know... *(Beat)* I suppose I have always wanted
to teach.

EMMELINE Teaching is far too taxing for a young woman of
your nervous disposition. A more contemplative environment
would better suit you. *(Beat)* You enjoy gardening, do you
not? *(Silence)* Good. It is settled then. After your return
from Scotland you will train to become a gardener. I have
contacts at Studley Horticultural College in Warwickshire.
We shall send you there.

EMMELINE *begins to put on her gloves.*

ADELA Don't leave...

EMMELINE The police have raided our offices in London and confiscated sackfuls of important documents. They intend to seize our funds. One way or another they intend to break us.

ADELA Let me come home with you...

EMMELINE No, that would not be a good idea.

EMMELINE *starts to exit.*

ADELA *(desperate)* Surely you need me...for the sake of the cause?

EMMELINE You will not be returning to work with the WSPU.

ADELA But it has been my entire life...

EMMELINE Your condition is too fragile.

ADELA I am a good public speaker...you have told me so yourself...

EMMELINE The WSPU has decided you will not speak again in public.

ADELA I am a Pankhurst....

EMMELINE The decision is final and not for debate. You will go to Studley where you will train as a gardener. You will never again make any public utterances on behalf of the WSPU. *(Beat. She softens)* Believe me child, it is all for the best.

EMMELINE *kisses* **ADELA** *and goes.* **ADELA** *is devastated, bewildered and alone. Music 17.*

MUSIC 17: ADELA'S REPRISE

ADELA

WHERE DID THE FUTURE GO?
ASPIRATIONS STOLE AWAY
THE PAST THAT BROUGHT ME HERE SEEMS TO THINK
THAT I'VE OUTSTAYED MY WELCOME.

Music 17 out. Lights fade on **ADELA**.

Scene Twelve

HARRY *in a bath chair. He is barely conscious. A sheet of paper lies in his lap.*

SYLVIA Poliomyelitis.

HELEN Polio.

SYLVIA Infantile paralysis.

HELEN It has been confirmed?

SYLVIA Yes. *(Beat)* Harry was out in the garden when he began to complain of headaches, muscle pains and sudden fevers.

HELEN But Harry is an adult...surely he will recover?

SYLVIA The prognosis is very bleak indeed. *(Beat)* The doctors say there is nothing more that can be done for him. *(Beat)* If he had contracted polio when he was a child the chances are that he might have survived...but in this case... *(Pause)* Harry is dying.

SYLVIA *embraces* **HELEN.** *Music 18.*

MUSIC 18: A LOVE AFFAIR

Music 18 under.

(taking the sheet of paper from **HARRY***)* Listen...he wrote this poem for you. (**SYLVIA** *reads)*

I saw thee, beloved,

And having seen thee, shall ever see,

I am a Greek, and thou,

O, Helen, within the walls of Troy.

Tell me, is there no weak spot,

In this great wall by which

I shall come to thee, beloved?

(**SYLVIA** *gives* **HELEN** *the poem)* He loves you. (**HELEN** *is upset)* Helen, I know you don't feel the same...can't feel the same for him...but you are the only love Harry has ever known. *(Beat)* Stay with him now. Hold his hand. Comfort him.

SYLVIA *leaves.* **HELEN** *holds* **HARRY***'s hand.*

HELEN I saw thee, beloved,

And having seen thee, shall ever see...

Music 18 up.

HARRY *opens his eyes.*

HARRY

THERE SHE IS AGAIN – STANDING AT MY BED
DO I HALLUCINATE A SCENE SEE VISIONS IN MY HEAD?
WELL A DREAM OR NOT
FEEL MY HEART REFER AS I RECALL THAT SPECIAL
DAY I FIRST SET EYES ON HER

HELEN

HARRY – THIS ISN'T A DREAM I'M BY YOUR SIDE
BUT HARRY – I WISH YOU TOLD ME HOW YOU FELT
NOT SIMPLY HIDE
BECAUSE I THINK I FEEL THE SAME – BUT JUST
DENIED IT FROM THE START
WHEN I HEARD YOU FIRST SAY MY NAME – FELT
SOMETHING CHANGE WITHIN MY HEART
YOU ARE THE ONE FOR ME.
YOU ARE MY DESTINY.

Music 18 under.

Lights come up on **ANNIE** *and* **CHRISTABEL**. **CHRISTABEL** *is writing.* **ANNIE** *stands behind her.* **ANNIE** *gently caresses* **CHRISTABEL***'s neck.* **CHRISTABEL** *moves her head away.*

CHRISTABEL I am working on my speech.

ANNIE You work all the hours God sends. You will burn yourself out.

CHRISTABEL A leader must lead.

ANNIE Won't you take a stroll with me, Christabel? It is such a beautiful day. The sun is shining and the roses are blooming.

CHRISTABEL Later.

Pause. **CHRISTABEL** *continues to write.*

ANNIE *kisses* **CHRISTABEL** *gently on the lips.*

Music 18 up.

LET'S PRETEND THAT DIDN'T HAPPEN

ANNIE
GREAT DENY THE WAY YOU FEEL
SAPPHIC LOVE IS ALL AROUND US
CHRISTABEL IT'S NO BIG DEAL

CHRISTABEL
I DON'T CARE THAT YOU'RE A WOMAN
I WAS BORN TO BE ALONE

ANNIE
THERE WE HAVE THE REAL ISSUE – ONE GREAT WALL... ONE
    HEART OF STONE

BUT CHRISTABEL I LOVE YOU – DENY IT IF YOU MUST.
BUT I'M BEGGING YOU FOR MERCY AND IN MY LOVE JUST
    TRUST

HARRY
LET'S MAKE PLANS ABOUT OUR FUTURE – LET'S NOT WASTE
    A MOMENT MORE

HELEN
HARRY WAIT

HARRY
PLEASE NOT A WORD NOW – SEE A FAITH YOU HAVE RESTORED

HELEN

    SO THE PLAN?

HARRY

    WE'LL HAVE A FAMILY – FATHER, MOTHER, DAUGHTER, SON

HELEN

    THAT'S THE PERFECT COMBINATION

HARRY

    YOU GO NEXT – I'VE JUST BEGUN

HELEN

    WE'LL GO TRAVELLING – A REAL ITALIAN HOLIDAY
    TO NAPLES, VENICE THEN POMPEII – A TRUE RENAISSANCE
      TRIP

HARRY

    FUTURE MEMORIES – ROMANTIC NOTIONS COMING TRUE
    LIVING OUT THE DREAM BECAUSE I'LL SEE IT ALL WITH YOU

BOTH

    DREAMS COMING TRUE

    Music 18 under.

ANNIE The sunset is lovely. Come and look.

CHRISTABEL You are very dear to me, Annie. But…

ANNIE Hold my hand.

    CHRISTABEL *does not move.*

    Music 18 up.

    CHRISTABEL I NEED YOU AND I KNOW YOU NEED ME TOO
    WHY DON'T YOU OPEN UP YOUR HEART –
    ACKNOWLEDGE FEELINGS STRONG AND TRUE?

CHRISTABEL

    ANNIE LOOK I'M REALLY FLATTERED THAT YOU FEEL THE
      WAY YOU DO

BUT IN CASE YOU HAVE FORGOTTEN – THERE'S A GOAL THAT
    I PURSUE
I CAN'T HANDLE MY EMOTIONS – SO I LOCK THEM DEEP
    INSIDE
THE FIGHT IS WHAT I LIVE FOR

ANNIE

GO AHEAD JUST RUN AND HIDE
BUT CHRISTABEL I WANT YOU – MELT THE WALL
AROUND YOUR HEART

CHRISTABEL

ANNIE I'M SO FRIGHTENED

ANNIE

TO ADMIT IT IS THE START

ALL FOUR

MY DARLING
THIS ISN'T A DREAM I'M BY YOUR SIDE MY DARLING
I WISH YOU TOLD ME HOW YOU FELT – NOT RUN AND HIDE
BECAUSE I KNOW I FEEL THE SAME – BUT JUST DENIED IT
    FROM THE START
WHEN I HEARD YOU FIRST SAY MY NAME – FELT SOMETHING
    CHANGE WITHIN MY HEART
YOU ARE THE ONE FOR ME.

ANNIE, CHRISTABEL *and* **HELEN**

YOU ARE MY DESTINY

HARRY *falls unconscious. Music 18 out.*

HELEN *(calling)* Sylvia… Christabel…help!

SYLVIA *and* **EMMELINE** *rush to* **HARRY**. *They are joined by* **CHRISTABEL** *and* **ANNIE**.

SYLVIA Harry…

EMMELINE My darling, lovely boy. What I have done to you.

HELEN *(kissing* **HARRY***)* Goodbye, Harry.

The stage fills with the opponents of the WSPU,
POLITICIANS, POLICE, MEN *and* **WOMEN.** *Music 19.*
Other **MEMBERS OF THE WSPU** *enter. The two sides face*
each other.

MUSIC 19: THE FORCES OF REACTION

MEN *and* **OTHERS**

> EVERY DAY THEY ESCALATE THEIR ACTION
> THINKING THAT WE'LL JUST GIVE IN
> WE'VE HUMOURED THEM FOR FAR TOO LONG
> BUT COMMON SENSE MUST SURELY WIN
>
> WOMEN WERE DESIGNED TO NURTURE
> MEN ARE HERE TO DO THE REST
> IT'S TIME TO GO BACK TO YOUR FAMILIES
> KNOWING THAT YOU DID YOUR BEST
>
> IT'S TIME TO TEACH THOSE SUFFRAGETTES A LESSON
> OUR SYMPATHY'S ALL GONE THEY WENT TOO FAR
> TILL NOW WE'VE PUT IT DOWN TO SELF EXPRESSION
> BUT NOW WE RUN THE RISK OF LEAVING A DEEP SCAR
> ON OUR GREAT NATION

CHRISTABEL

> TOO MUCH TO BEAR
> I HEAR THE VOICES ALL AROUND ME FORCE MYSELF TO CARE
> BUT THE PRESSURE'S BUILDING UP
> I FEEL MY HEARTBEAT RACE
> I SEE HARRY'S FACE
> REMEMBER PROMISES NOW BROKE
> A RELENTLESS GAME WITH A THWARTED AIM
> I CAN'T GO ON

CHRISTABEL, *unable to bear any longer the strain of*
leadership, slips away.

MEN *and* **OTHERS**

> BY RAMMING ISSUES DOWN OUR THROAT
> PROTESTING FOR THE RIGHT TO VOTE
> THEY'VE UNDERMINED THEIR ARGUMENT

AND PROVED THEY'RE NOT EQUIPPED
WITH RATIONAL, INTELLIGENCE
USING VIOLENCE GIVES THEM NO DEFENCE
IT'S TIME TO SORT THEM OUT BEFORE THE NATION'S HEART
    IS RIPPED

Music 19 under.

ANNIE One day we will triumph, Christabel. I know we will.
We will have changed the world. You will have changed
the world. *(Beat)* Christabel? Christabel? *(Realising*
CHRISTABEL *has gone)* Where are you, Christabel? Where
have you gone?

Music up. The forces opposing the **WSPU** *exit.*

ALL

WE'VE LISTENED AND BEEN PATRONISED
BUT NOW IT'S TIME TO MOBILISE THE POLICE AND TURN THE
    HEAT UP WE'RE NO LONGER HOLDING BACK

WSPU

OUR LEADER'S GONE, NOW WHAT TO DO?
I THINK THE PRESSURE'S NOW ON YOU
OUR PATIENCE HAS NOW ENDED
WARNING GIVEN
WE ATTACK

Music 19 out.

FLORA Where is Christabel?

ANNIE She had to go. Don't you see? The police would have
arrested her and God knows what might have happened then.

TERESSA Has Christabel left us?

ANNIE She had no choice. She's our figurehead. Our leader.
(Beat) She's still with us in spirit. Can't you feel her? She's
standing right here beside us.

Scene Thirteen

Paris. The salon of the PRINCESSE DE POLIGNAC.

Sound effects: a gramophone playing the end of *"ALEXANDER'S RAGTIME BAND".*

CHRISTABEL *and the* PRINCESSE *laugh as they dance. Record comes to an end.*

Sound effects out.

PRINCESSE Get your coat. Picasso's new exhibition opens today and the whole world will be there.

CHRISTABEL All those distorted shapes...is it really art?

PRINCESSE Of course it's art. Great art. New art. Picasso is a genius! You have so much to unlearn, Christabel Pankhurst.

CHRISTABEL It's so different here in Paris...with you.

PRINCESSE You don't like it?

CHRISTABEL I love it. London's stuffy. Cobwebs everywhere. Here I feel free. For the first time in my life I feel like me.

PRINCESSE Every woman should be free.

CHRISTABEL I've never enjoyed myself so much. Never laughed so much. Thank you.

PRINCESSE Tonight, my dear, we will attend the Ballets Russe where you will meet the great Stravinsky himself. *(Beat)* After the ballet I think a visit to the Folie Bergère. Mistinguett herself is appearing. *(Beat)* Why the sudden sadness?

CHRISTABEL Guilt.

PRINCESSE What have you to feel guilty about?

CHRISTABEL Disappearing like I did. Running away to Paris. Leaving the WSPU in the lurch.

PRINCESSE You had no choice. If you had remained in London you'd be in a prison cell by now. You've served the cause nobly, my darling. Let others do their bit. *(Beat)* High time to let your hair down. Enjoy Paris and everything she has to offer.

CHRISTABEL Everything.

PRINCESSE Everything.

The two **WOMEN** *embrace.* **ANNIE** *enters.*

MUSIC 20: "TELL ME".

CHRISTABEL
> PIROUETTES AND ARABESQUES, TRANSPORT ME TO AN AGE –
>> WHERE A YOUNG GIRL'S ASPIRATIONS WERE RIGHT THERE UP ON THE STAGE
> INSTEAD I JUST COMPLIED
> WATCH THE GIRL AS SHE JUST DIED
> NOW I'M STANDING HERE WITH YOU RIGHT BY MY SIDE

PRINCESSE
> TELL ME HOW YOU FEEL?

CHRISTABEL
> I FEEL SCARED AND I FEEL FREE

PRINCESSE
> WE'D SAY C'EST LA VIE

CHRISTABEL
> ALRIGHT FOR YOU BUT NOT FOR ME

PRINCESSE
> TELL ME WHAT YOU WANT?

CHRISTABEL
> SOME BREATHING SPACE... SOME AIR
> SOME TIME FOR ME
> THAT'S A LIFE I COULD SHARE
>
> BUT I DON'T KNOW HOW TO DO 'THIS'

PRINCESSE
> WHAT IS 'THIS'?

CHRISTABEL
> I JUST DON'T KNOW
> FEEL I NEED YOUR ARMS AROUND ME

PRINCESSE
> WELL?

CHRISTABEL
> DO I DARE, OR WOULD YOU GO?

PRINCESSE
> THIS IS YOUR TIME TO BE SELFISH
> IT'S YOUR TURN TO MEET YOUR NEEDS
> TIME TO FIGHT YOUR PRIVATE DEMONS
> TURN DESIRE INTO DEEDS
>
> TAKE MY HAND – YOU'RE STOOD THERE SHAKING
> THERE'S NO NEED TO BE AFRAID
> AS I FEEL THE SAME AS YOU DO
> NEW SENSATIONS DO PERVADE

BOTH
> LET'S TAKE PLEASURE IN THIS MOMENT
> HERE TOGETHER, ALL ALONE
> MAYBE DESTINY HAS SPOKEN
> AS I TAKE YOU FOR MY OWN

During song **ANNIE** *enters. Neither* **CHRISTABEL** *or the* **PRINCESSE** *notice* **ANNIE** *and at the end, both fall into a longing kiss, only to be interrupted.*

Music 20 out.

ANNIE The maid let me in. *(Beat)* No one followed me.

ANNIE *tries to embrace* **CHRISTABEL**, *who pulls away from her.*

CHRISTABEL Why have you followed me here?

ANNIE Everyone at home wants to know how you are. *(Beat)* They worry about you. *(Beat)* I worry about you.

PRINCESSE Who is this woman?

CHRISTABEL Annie Kenney.

PRINCESSE The mill girl.

ANNIE The mill girl. *(Beat)* Who the hell are you?

PRINCESSE I am the Princesse de Polignac.

ANNIE But you're...

PRINCESSE An American. Correct. The title came with my marriage. I've grown used to it. (ANNIE *looks from the* PRINCESSE *to* CHRISTABEL. *She cannot understand)* Mine is a marriage of convenience. My husband prefers the company of young men and I prefer the company of brilliant and beautiful women.

Silence.

CHRISTABEL What news?

ANNIE Helen Craggs got nine months for attempted arson. A suffragette called Mary Leigh attempted to attack Asquith with an axe.

CHRISTABEL Foolhardy...

PRINCESSE She should have chopped off his head!

ANNIE Then she and Gladys Evans tried to burn down a theatre where Asquith was watching a performance...

The PRINCESSE *laughs.*

CHRISTABEL *(irritated)* And...

ANNIE Five years. They're on hunger strike. Emily Wilding Davison has become a law unto herself... Pansy is not at all well, her nerves are shattered...some of them are saying that we need to commit to greater militancy, others argue the opposite case...several wealthy ladies have withdrawn their support...everyone is at each other's throats.

CHRISTABEL I gave you complete power to lead the WSPU as you thought fit. Now there appears to be anarchy.

ANNIE Because they want you to lead them. They're desperate for you to return. They'll obey you. *(Beat)*. Please come home, Christabel.

Pause.

CHRISTABEL Are my sisters behaving themselves?

ANNIE Adela is gardening.

CHRISTABEL And Sylvia?

ANNIE Stirring up trouble in the East End...

CHRISTABEL My mother?

ANNIE She continues with her hunger strike in Holloway Prison. *(Beat)* By all accounts she is fading fast. *(Beat)* Come home before it is too late.

Pause.

CHRISTABEL I will contact you when the time is right for my return.

PRINCESSE We're late for the opening of the exhibition. *(To* ANNIE*)* My maid will see you out.

CHRISTABEL I will return, Annie. One day I will return. Tell them that.

CHRISTABEL *and the* PRINCESSE *leave.*

MUSIC 21: "HOLD MY HAND" – REPRISE

ANNIE
THE CONSTANT BEAT MADE STRONGER IN YOUR PRESENCE
EACH BREATH I TAKE IS DEEPER COS YOU'RE NEAR
I'M SMITTEN BY YOUR CHARMS
I HAVE NO DEFENCE
UNTIL YOU FEEL THE SAME I...

Breaks down.

Scene Fourteen

FLORA, GRACE, PANSY, HELEN, EMILY *and* OTHER WSPU WOMEN *enter and immediately start an impassioned argument about what they should do next.* ANNIE *enters and watches them.*

PANSY When will Christabel return?

FLORA We are an army without a leader.

GRACE When?

HELEN It must be soon. We can't go on like this.

EMILY She has deserted us.

ANNIE *(turning on* EMILY*)* Christabel would never desert us! She had no choice but to flee to Paris. They want to make an example of her. *(Beat)* Christabel's heart is here... here with the WSPU. *(Beat)* When the time is right she will return.

Spotlight comes up on the JUDGE. *The* WOMEN *watch.*

JUDGE Bring the defendant forward. *(*EMMELINE *staggers into the courtroom. She is extremely frail and near death)* Emmeline Pankhurst you been found guilty on fifty-four counts of conspiracy. Have you anything to say for yourself?

EMMELINE What right have you, as a man, to judge women? We women have no voice in saying what is a crime and what is not a crime!

JUDGE Silence! *(Beat)* Your seditious and evil ideas have destroyed homes and broken marriages. You have poisoned the minds of tens of thousands of innocent and suggestible women. You have brought this great nation to the edge of anarchy. *(Beat)* You will serve nine months in prison. *(Desperate protests from the* WSPU*)* Silence! Take her down.

Music 22.

MUSIC 22: MY DAY

INSUFFERABLE THESE SUFFRAGETTES SHOULD BE
    IMPRISONED TILL THEY DIE
THEY PLAY AT HUNGER STRIKING FOR THEIR CAUSE TO
    MAGNIFY
BUT WE RELEASE THEM FAR TOO EARLY SO THEY FIGHT
    ANOTHER DAY
I LACK JOB SATISFACTION TILL I'VE LOCKED THEM ALL AWAY

ADELA *appears. She is on the verge of a breakdown.
All parts keep singing.* **JUDGE** *repeats the above verse
simultaneous with* **EMMELINE.**

EMMELINE

ONE MORE DAY INCARCERATED IS I SUSPECT A DAY TOO
    LONG
NEVER HAVE I FELT MORE SCARED WHEN IN THE PAST I'VE
    FELT SO STRONG
BUT PUT ME IN YOUR PRISONS AS ALL OUR OPTIONS
    DISAPPEAR
I JUST WISH I DIDN'T HAVE A SENSE OF ALL CONSUMING
    FEAR
WISH I DIDN'T HAVE A SENSE OF ALL CONSUMING FEAR

ADELA

HUSH ADELA, NO ADELA
THANK YOU CHRISTABEL AND MOTHER – MY DAY HAS COME
OSTRACISED AND PATRONISED NO MORE WITH OTHER
EYES I SEE HOW THINGS SHOULD BE DONE
NO MORE YOUNGEST DAUGHTER NOW A WOMAN WITH AN
    AIM
TIME TO CHANGE THE RULES WITHIN THE PANKHURST
    FAMILY GAME

As **JUDGE** *and* **ADELA, ANNIE** *and the* **WSPU** *repeat their
verses,* **EMMELINE** *sings over...*

WSPU

> YOU THOUGHT IF YOU IGNORED US WE'D PACK AND GO AWAY
> WE SAID IT ONCE BEFORE THE RIGHT TO VOTE IS HERE TO
>   STAY
> ESCALATE ACTIVITIES DESTRUCTION NOW OUR GOAL
> IT'S TIME TO FACE THE BATTLE LEAVE BEHIND OUR SELF
>   CONTROL *(Repeat)*

ALL

> THIS IS MY DAY

Music 22 out.

Scene Fifteen

Lights up on **CHRISTABEL** *in Paris, drinking wine with the* **PRINCESSE**.

PRINCESSE Did you ever see ballet like it? Outrageous. And that man Diaghilev...with that natty little moustache he looks more like a Wall Street broker than a ballet impresario... and Nijinsky...like a creature of the forest...a wolf...a faun... so lithe, beautiful and dangerous...

MUSIC 23: "CAN'T CARRY ON".

(beat) Have you heard a word I've said?

CHRISTABEL I beg your pardon?

PRINCESSE That girl Annie...her visit bothered you. Tell the truth.

CHRISTABEL
AS OFTEN WITH THE FIRST BORN I WAS THE FAVOURED CHILD
I LIVED THE LIFE MY MOTHER YEARNED TO ALL INTENTS
    BEGUILED
BUT I'M A LEADER OF A CAUSE THAT'S LOST
DIRECTION
STRONG WOMEN ALL BELIEVING THEY ARE RIGHT
BUT THE BURDEN IS TOO GREAT
FEEL MY RESOLVE DETERIORATE
LOST WHERE I BELONG
I CAN'T CARRY ON

Lights come up on **EMMELINE** *in her prison cell. She stirs.*

EMMELINE
WITH JUST THE SOUND OF MY HEART FOR COMPANY
IT'S A WEAKER BEAT RESOUND IN ME — I'M SLOWLY DYING IN
    THIS CELL
IMPRISONED IN THIS HELL
BUT NOW THE BODY'S WEAK - THE FLAME GROWS DIM
A MARTYR BORN FROM HEROINE

ABDICATE RESPONSIBILITY
BY FIGHTING FOR THE VOTE I FEEL LIKE I'VE LOST ME
LOST WHERE I BELONG
I CAN'T CARRY ON

PANSY

I SAID I'D BE HERE TIL THE END
IF THIS IS IT I CAN'T PRETEND THAT I'M NOT SCARED
SO UNPREPARED
IN THE BEGINNING I HAD AN AIM
AN INJUSTICE I COULD DECLAIM
A MORAL STANCE
A CAUSE TO ADVANCE
EVERY DAY THE FIGHT GETS HARDER
ONE BY ONE OUR WOMEN FELL
NOW IT'S MY TURN TO REFLECT, AS I FACE MY OWN FAREWELL
LOST WHERE I BELONG
I CAN'T CARRY ON

Lights come up on **ADELA** *who is planting seeds in a garden.*

ADELA

HOW DID I END UP HERE?
EACH DECISION CAUSED MORE PAIN
A FAMILY DISJOINTED FOR A GOAL SO UNOBTAINABLE
DELIBERATES, DISASSOCIATES
IT'S IN MYSELF I SHOULD BELIEVE

FOR THIS LAST DELIBERATION I'M REWARDED A REPRIEVE
LOST WHERE I BELONG
I CAN'T CARRY ON

Lights come up on **SYLVIA** *at her easel.*

SYLVIA

SEE EACH WOMAN'S STORY BY THE LINES ETCHED ON HER
    FACE
THE LINES ARE GETTING DEEPER AS HER HISTORY I RETRACE
EXHAUSTED BY THE BATTLE AS FATIGUE CONSUMES THE
    SOUL

IT'S A SACRIFICE MORE FUTILE IF THEY FAIL TO REACH THEIR
   GOAL
LOST WHERE I BELONG
THIS CAN'T GO ON

Lights come up **HELEN CRAGGS**. *She is reading* **HARRY***'s
poem.*

HELEN

HARRY LOOK AT ME
STAYED TRUE TO WHAT WE BOTH BELIEVED
OH WHY DID YOU DECIDE TO LEAVE
I KNOW YOU HAD NO CHOICE
IN MY HEART YOU LIVE
AND EVERY DAY I MISS YOU MORE
YOUR CONSTANT PRESENCE CAN'T IGNORE
THAT I CAN'T CARRY ON WITH YOU I BELONG

Lights come up on all **OTHER WSPU WOMEN**. *They are
exhausted and near defeat.*

ALL WSPU WOMEN

YOU THOUGHT IF YOU IGNORED US WE'D PACK UP AND GO
   AWAY?
DESPITE OUR MANY SETBACKS WE WILL FIGHT ANOTHER DAY
BUT FUNDS ARE RUNNING SHORT AND IN SOME AREAS EVEN
   GONE
WE NEED SOME BENEFACTORS OR WE'LL FAIL TO CARRY ON...

EMILY *breaks out of the* **WSPU WOMEN**.

Music 23 out.

*Sound effects: distant thundering of horses hooves on
turf. Thundering grows louder.*

Excited racegoers enter and watch the derby. **EMILY**
pushes her way to the front of the crowd at the racetrack.

1ST MAN Craganour's hitting the front...

2ND MAN Aboyeur's holding him...

3RD MAN Come on!

1ST MAN Come on!

2ND MAN Come on!

EMILY Votes for women!

2ND MAN Here comes Day Comet...

1ST MAN My money's on the king's mount!

2ND MAN Come on!

3RD MAN Come on!

1ST MAN Come on!

EMILY Votes for women.

1ST MAN Shut up you stupid woman!

EMILY Deeds not words!

> The MEN *continue to shout, their excitement growing. Their cries become louder and louder as the horses approach.*
>
> *Sound effects: the thunder of horses hooves reaches a deafening climax.*
>
> EMILY *runs onto the racetrack and stands in front of the oncoming horses. Then, simultaneously...*
>
> *Sound effects: thunder of horses hooves cuts.*
>
> *All shouting cuts.*
>
> *Lights snap out on* EMILY. EMMELINE, CHRISTABEL, SYLVIA, ADELA *and* ALL WSPU *sense something catastrophic has occurred.*
>
> *Lights come up on* EMILY *lying on the racetrack. She has been trampled to death. Music returns.*

Music 24.

MUSIC 24: A FRAGILE HEART

The **WSPU WOMEN** *sing a final chorus as they raise up*
EMILY's *body and drape it in the suffragette banner.*

WSPU

A FRAGILE HEART
REPERCUSSIONS UNFORESEEN WHEN AT THE START
LEFT TO LIVE WITH SILENT PAIN
WAS THIS DEATH TO BE IN VAIN
WE WON'T FORGET
REMORSE, REGRET

SO WITH PRIDE AND BANNERS HIGH
SUFFRAGETTES WE GLORIFY
PURPLE GREEN AND WHITE
COLOURS OF OUR FIGHT

THE RIGHTEOUS CAUSE CAN'T FAIL TO WIN TILL VICT'RY WE
    MUST FIGHT
STAND PROUDLY 'NEATH OUR STANDARD – THE PURPLE,
    GREEN AND WHITE
OUR STRENGTH STILL LIES IN NUMBERS
OUR ONLY OPTION NOW TO WIN
I STAND AMONGST MY SISTERS
EACH OF US A HEROINE

The **WSPU** *hum.*

The **WOMEN** *exit with the body of* **EMILY**.

Music 24 out.

Scene Sixteen

Sound effects: distant booming of heavy guns.

1914. The London offices of the **WSPU.** **MEMBERS OF THE WSPU** *congregate. Animated talk about the outbreak of war.*

FLORA Waterloo station's chock-a-block with khaki, all of 'em off to France.

ANNIE My sister's boy says he's joining up.

HELEN Damn this war.

GRACE It's all the newspapers can write about. War, war, war!

FLORA It's as if the WSPU never existed.

SYLVIA *and* **ADELA** *enter.*

ANNIE What are you two doing here?

SYLVIA Now war's been declared it's time to put aside our differences and stand together. WSPU, Labour Party...every sane person must stand up and oppose this unjust war.

ADELA I want to help... I want to be useful.

ANNIE Stay away from us. We don't need you. Neither of you.

SYLVIA Annie, stop and think. This war is wrong. It's a clash of empires. Britain, France, Germany, Russia, Austro-Hungry... kings, grand dukes, tsars...not ordinary people.

GRACE It's sure to be over soon enough then we can get back to campaigning for the cause.

ADELA You don't know that.

ANNIE Thought you were growing flowers these days.

ADELA Why do you hate me so?

ANNIE Don't hate you. But you've nothing to offer that we want.

Unseen by the others EMMELINE *and* CHRISTABEL *enter.* EMMELINE *is weak and frail.* CHRISTABEL *has just arrived back in London from Paris. She carries a suitcase.*

SYLVIA It is the duty of the WSPU to oppose this war with all the strength it can muster!

CHRISTABEL The WSPU will do nothing of the sort.

Overjoyed the WSPU WOMEN *flock to* CHRISTABEL.

EMMELINE Thank God my daughter has come home. *(Beat)* Remember, you speak not just for yourself or the WSPU...you speak for twenty million British women who have no voice.

CHRISTABEL *(to all)* From this moment forward the WSPU will give complete and total support to our government, support that will not waver until this war is won. All other activities will be suspended.

SYLVIA *(stunned)* You support this war?

CHRISTABEL We support the government and the people of Great Britain in the prosecution of this war.

SYLVIA In God's name, why?

CHRISTABEL In order to win women the vote.

ADELA I don't understand? Thousands will die...widows... orphans...

CHRISTABEL Blood will not be shed in vain. Out of sacrifice will come not only victory over the kaiser but our reward for patriotic support. The government will not be able to refuse women the right to vote.

SYLVIA You'd buy the vote with gravestones?

CHRISTABEL If that's what it takes. Thousands of gravestones. Millions even.

SYLVIA What have you become?

CHRISTABEL Sylvia, you are expelled from the WSPU.

SYLVIA You can't do that!

ANNIE We all stand behind Christabel. You are expelled.

SYLVIA Mother...

EMMELINE *says nothing.*

CHRISTABEL Adela, you will embark for Australia at the earliest possible opportunity...

ADELA No...let me stay here...let be stand beside you...

CHRISTABEL Impossible. It is better that you are kept out of the way.

SYLVIA We are your own flesh and blood. *(To* **CHRISTABEL***)* We are sisters.

MUSIC NO 25 "FINALE" starts.

CHRISTABEL Flesh and blood count for nothing now. For this cause I will sacrifice anything. Family...love...happiness... what do they matter beside the great prize...the emancipation of women. *(Beat)* I am nothing. We are all nothing. Our lives have but one single, unalterable purpose. What becomes of me...what becomes of any of us...does not matter...cannot matter. *(Beat)* Our little lives are set against the lives of millions of women today and in the future.

ANNIE Don't say that, Christabel. You matter. Love matters.

CHRISTABEL It is already said. *(Beat)* It is too late to change history.

CHRISTABEL, **SYLVIA** *and* **ADELA** *all mount soapboxes. They speak directly to the audience. During the song other characters from the play appear, including the ghosts of* **HARRY** *and* **EMILY***.*

CHRISTABEL

CHRISTABEL

SYLVIA
> SYLVIA

ADELA
> ADELA

ALL THREE
> PANKHURST THROUGH AND THROUGH
> THREE DAUGHTERS BORN TO GREATNESS – TO STAGE A
>   SOCIAL COUP
> EACH FIGHT WILL BE RECORDED FOR ALL THE WORLD TO SEE
> HOW WE THE PANKHURST SISTERS EARNED OUR PLACE IN
>   HISTORY
>
> BUT NEW DREAMS ARE CREATED BY EVENTS THAT JUST
>   APPEAR
> WE RE-EVALUATE OUR MISSIONS WITH A CONSCIENCE NOW
>   MORE CLEAR

Music 25 under. A **YOUNG MAN** *enters.* **CHRISTABEL**
hands him a white feather.

1ST MAN Take this back! I'm no bloody shirker!

CHRISTABEL Then why aren't you in uniform?

1ST MAN I was wounded at Passchendaele...

Music 25 up.

CHRISTABEL You look fit enough to me!

> WE'VE A DUTY TO OUR COUNTRY TO DEFEND OUR LIBERTY
> OUR MEN SHOULD BE SUPPORTED AS THEY FIGHT WITH
>   BRAVERY
> ALL WOMEN SHOULD SUPPORT THEM UNTIL THIS WAR IS
>   THROUGH
> THEN WE WILL BE REWARDED – IT'S THE RIGHTEOUS THING
>   TO DO

SYLVIA
> WE FIGHT FOR SOCIAL JUSTICE – FOR A BATTLE JUST TO LIVE
> WE URGE THE RICH AMONGST YOU TO GENEROUSLY GIVE

A DIVISION OF THE RICHES – SOCIALISM IS THE WAY
EQUALITY FOR ALL
THE WEALTHY HAVE TO PAY

ADELA

I SPEAK FROM MY EXPERIENCE THAT IN WAR NO ONE CAN
WIN
SO PEOPLE OF AUSTRALIA THIS IS WHERE I SHALL BEGIN
TO CHANGE THE CURRENT THINKING – THAT TO FIGHT'S THE
ONLY WAY
A WORLD IN ARBITRATION IS A WORLD I CHOSE TODAY

CHRISTABEL November 1918. The Great War ends. Parliament
passes the act that gives women the vote.

FULL COMPANY

JUST AN EVERYDAY DESCRIPTION OF A FAMILY AT WAR
WE NEVER COULD HAVE GUESSED JUST WHAT THE FUTURE
HELD IN STORE
FAMILIAL SCRIPT RE-WRITTEN – A NEW CHAPTER EACH
BEGINS
BUT THE BATTLE STILL UNNAMED

CHRISTABEL *steps forward.*

The **WOMEN** *celebrate. Celebrations suddenly freeze.*
ANNIE *steps forward.*

ANNIE Christabel...hold my hand. *(Is ignored)*

Music 25 comes back up.

ALL

IS THE PRIVATE ONE WITHIN (**EMILY** *walks through the
suffragettes in modern-day dress – holding up a ballot
paper.)*

End of show

FURNITURE AND PROPERTY LIST

ACT I

Scene Two

Tea tray
Tea pot
Milk jug
Garibaldis
Biscuit plate
Tea cups
Tea saucers
Tea spoons
Chairs
Pen
Writing paper

Scene Seven

Daily Mail newspaper
Pen
Writing paper
Sashes
Stones
Chain

Scene Eight

Chalk

Scene Nine

Sashes
Sticks
Clubs
Stones
Metal prison plates
Feeding tube
Feeding funnel
Feeding jug

ACT II

Scene Ten

Champagne bottle
Champagne glasses
The Times newspaper
Rope
Chains

Scene Eleven

Suitcase (**Adela**)
Garibaldis

Scene Twelve

Gloves (**Emmeline**)

Scene Thirteen

Bath chair
Poem
Writing paper
Pen

Scene Fourteen

Gramaphone

Scene Sixteen

Bottle of French wine
Wine glasses
Seeds
Easel
Poem
Banner

Scene Seventeen

Suitcase (**Christabel**)
Soap boxes
White feather

Lightning Source UK Ltd.
Milton Keynes UK
UKHW02f2120120618
324135UK00006B/553/P